"Never resorting to overbearin¡
Walls provides readers with insights that are clear, concise, and
penetrating. He sorts through the various stances on a number
of issues related to the afterlife in a way that is respectful and
courteous. This book, which makes the afterlife as solid and as
real as this life—not stiff, sentimental, or founded upon fear—
will be a more than welcome addition to a Christian's library."

—**Devin Brown**, author of *A Life Observed: A Spiritual
Biography of C. S. Lewis*

"Jerry Walls offers an insightful, accessible defense of heaven,
hell, and purgatory. Though still unpersuaded about the latter,
I would urge the reading of this book, first, for the important
theological and philosophical insights it affords concerning hell
(the realm of the illusory triumph of the creature's will) and
heaven (the new, transformed—though still physical—earth
and heaven that are permeated by God's presence and blessing); indeed, much wisdom on these doctrines alone is to be
found herein. Second, concerning purgatory, Protestants have a
unique opportunity to more fully understand the arguments for
and then to properly assess the merits (!) of this doctrine. The
book is sure to generate much lively discussion and deepened
understanding."

—**Paul Copan**, Palm Beach Atlantic University

"Jerry Walls shows once again that on the four last things—
death, judgment, hell, and heaven—he is by far the most thoughtful evangelical philosopher. His mastery of Scripture, historical
theology, and the philosophical literature is unmatched."

—**Francis J. Beckwith**, Baylor University

HEAVEN, HELL, AND PURGATORY

RETHINKING THE THINGS THAT MATTER MOST

JERRY L. WALLS

BrazosPress
a division of Baker Publishing Group
Grand Rapids, Michigan

© 2015 by Jerry L. Walls

Published by Brazos Press
a division of Baker Publishing Group
P.O. Box 6287, Grand Rapids, MI 49516-6287
www.brazospress.com

Printed in the United States of America

Library of Congress Cataloging-in-Publication Data
Walls, Jerry L.
Heaven, Hell, and Purgatory : rethinking the things that matter most / Jerry L. Walls.
    pages cm
Includes bibliographical references and index.
ISBN 978-1-58743-356-6 (pbk.)
    1. Future life—Christianity. 2. Heaven—Christianity. 3. Hell—Christianity.
4. Purgatory. I. Title.
BT903.W35 2015
236'.2—dc23   2014032342

Unless noted otherwise, Scripture quotations are from the 1984 edition of the Holy Bible, New International Version®. NIV®. Copyright © 1973, 1978, 1984, 2011 by Biblica, Inc.™ Used by permission of Zondervan. All rights reserved worldwide. www.zondervan.com

Scripture quotations labeled NRSV are from the New Revised Standard Version of the Bible, copyright © 1989, by the Division of Christian Education of the National Council of the Churches of Christ in the United States of America. Used by permission. All rights reserved.

15   16   17   18   19   20   21   7   6   5   4   3   2   1

To Beatrice

"She, with a smile that left my faculties
Quite vanquished, said to me:
'Turn and give heed;
Not in my eyes alone is Paradise.'"

—Dante

CONTENTS

Acknowledgments 9

Introduction 11

1. Heaven, Trinity, and the Meaning of Life 19

2. Consolation Measures When the Dream Has Died 47

3. If God Is Love, Why Is There a Hell? 67

4. If We Are Saved by Grace, Why Do We Need
   Purgatory? 91

5. Saving Souls and/or Bodies: Personal Identity in the
   Afterlife 117

6. Wiping Away Every Tear? The Afterlife and the Problem
   of Evil 139

7. Ultimate Motivation: Heaven, Hell, and the Ground
   of Morality 163

8. His Mercy Endures Forever—Even beyond the
   Grave? 187

Conclusion: "Can You Believe It?" 213

Notes 221

Index 231

ACKNOWLEDGMENTS

I am happy to acknowledge several people who helped in the writing of this book. Karla Estrada read the entire manuscript chapter by chapter as I was writing it and offered many encouraging comments and helpful suggestions. Luke Van Horn also read several chapters and provided several critical comments that helped me clarify my arguments at a number of points. I remain ever thankful to my PhD mentor at Notre Dame, Tom Morris, whose impact on my thinking and philosophical development continues to influence everything I write. I am also thankful for my colleagues at Houston Baptist University. HBU is a great place to teach and do serious Christian scholarship, and I appreciate the encouragement and support for my writing projects from both faculty colleagues and the administration. And finally, I must thank my children, Timothy and Angela Amos and Jonathan and Emily Walls, and my granddaughters, Madelyn Rose and Mackenzie Grace Amos. They too influence everything I write by the many ways they portend heaven.

INTRODUCTION

The immortality of the soul is something of such vital importance to us, affecting us so deeply, that one must have lost all feeling not to care about knowing the facts of the matter. All our actions and thoughts must follow such different paths according to whether there is hope of eternal blessings or not, that the only possible way of acting with sense and judgment is to decide our course in light of this point, which ought to be our ultimate objective.

—Pascal[1]

This book deals with the most important questions you will ever think about, questions that every sane person must care about. You can deny that heaven and hell are real, but you cannot rationally be indifferent about the matter. Given what is at stake, the only sensible attitude is to care, and to care deeply.

The Christian doctrines of the afterlife have undoubtedly had an enormous impact on Western culture and have inspired everything from classic art and literature to the everyday hopes and fears of countless people. However, these doctrines have been under attack to one degree or another ever since the onset of the modern period, when a number of influential thinkers began to call them into question as part of a more general rejection of traditional religious belief.

Hell Disappeared; Heaven Too?

In more recent times, many intellectuals, even theologians, have suggested that heaven is nothing more than a fading memory and that the flames of hell have flickered out. Just a few decades ago, in 1985, the noted religious historian Martin E. Marty published an article entitled "Hell Disappeared. No One Noticed. A Civic Argument."[2] One of the telling claims of his article was that he did a bibliographical search for recent material about hell but could find almost nothing. No one, it seemed, still believed in hell or thought much about it anymore. A few years later, in 1989, in an article in *Newsweek*, Harvard theologian Gordon Kaufman, citing what he saw as "irreversible changes," declared, "I don't think there can be any future for heaven and hell."[3]

Just two years later, however, *US News and World Report* did a cover story entitled "Hell's Sober Comeback" in which it reported a revival of belief in the doctrine, even among theologians. At the time, I had just written a dissertation defending the doctrine of hell for my PhD in philosophy at Notre Dame; that dissertation was published in 1992. The next year, two more books on hell were published by major university presses.[4] Anyone who has been paying attention knows that hell has moved back to the front burner in the past few decades, and if Marty were doing a bibliographical search today, he would have no problem finding ample material.

Indeed, the doctrine of hell is a matter of intense debate at the current time, especially in evangelical Protestant circles. Some are defending traditional views of literal physical punishment, others are interpreting the torment of hell more metaphorically, and still others are arguing that the wicked will be annihilated rather than punished forever. More recently still, a number of theologians and philosophers have been arguing for universal salvation and denying that any are lost forever.[5]

A good measure of contemporary interest in these issues was the heated controversy that erupted over heaven and hell when Rob Bell's 2011 book *Love Wins* was the subject of acrimonious internet warfare before it was even published.[6] Rumor had it that Bell was advocating universalism, denying hell, and the like. So volatile was the controversy that the cover of *Time* magazine posed the question, "What If There's No Hell?"[7] Underneath the word "Hell" in large red letters, the cover read: "A popular pastor's best-selling book has stirred fierce debate about sin, salvation, and judgment."

Contrary to Marty's claim, interest in hell never disappeared after all, and indeed, it appears to be back with a vengeance.

Nor has interest in heaven waned, contrary to Kaufman's pronouncement in *Newsweek*. Indeed, Lisa Miller, for several years the religion editor of that magazine, published a book in 2010 with a title that takes on a certain ironic twist in light of Kaufman's prediction, namely, *Heaven: Our Enduring Fascination with the Afterlife*. Miller notes that belief in the afterlife has been on the rise lately, with a 2007 Gallup poll indicating that 81 percent of Americans claimed to believe in heaven, up from 72 percent in 1997.[8]

Contemporary interest in the afterlife is also apparent in the extraordinary success of books about heaven written by people who have "died" or had near-death experiences in which they claimed to visit the heavenly realm. An enormously popular example is *Heaven Is for Real: A Little Boy's Astounding Story of His Trip to Heaven and Back*,[9] which was also made into a movie that was a box-office hit in 2014. As I write these lines, the most recent such bestseller is *Proof of Heaven: A Neurosurgeon's Journey into the Afterlife*.[10] Such books have the additional appeal of grounding the hope of the afterlife in empirical or scientific data. What they undeniably demonstrate, however, is our ongoing fascination with the glimpses (and in some cases extended visions) of the afterlife that they purport to provide.

More Than Fascination

But I want to emphasize that there is far more involved here than mere fascination. Indeed, fascination can be nothing more than curiosity at the unusual or the entertaining, the mysterious, and even the bizarre. Certainly, much that is written about heaven and hell is sensational and appeals to these tendencies. Moreover, popular writing about the afterlife is often sentimental, simplistic, and emotionally manipulative.

There is no doubt that some—perhaps much—of the continuing fascination with the afterlife is of the sensational and sentimental variety. It is the same sort of fascination some have with UFOs, ghost stories, and vampire romance novels.

But there is a much deeper reason we cannot look away, and that is simply because we have an enormous personal stake in these issues. Again, as I said at the outset, you cannot rationally be indifferent to heaven and hell. Blaise Pascal, the seventeenth-century philosopher, mathematician, and all-around genius, made this point with characteristically pointed passion in a number of passages, such as the one I quoted at the beginning of this introduction.[11] As Pascal notes, there are vast and far-reaching consequences for both our thoughts and our actions, depending on whether our lives will end after several decades or go on forever. Simply put, the Christian doctrines of the afterlife involve a set of profoundly substantive truth claims with explosive implications.

I have been thinking about these extraordinary truth claims and their explosive implications throughout my academic career and, indeed, for several years before I ever went to graduate school to study philosophy. I was raised in a small, rural church in southern Ohio where the Christian version of the cosmic drama, complete with resurrection, final judgment, and heaven and hell, was passionately communicated in the preaching and teaching. Listening to the sermons at Bethel Chapel, one knew that matters of life and death and eternal happiness or misery were at stake in how one responded to the gospel.

All of this was called into question for me, however, when I went to Princeton Seminary to study theology. Not everyone I encountered there believed in the afterlife, let alone the traditional Christian account of it, and I particularly recall that the doctrine of hell was sharply challenged not only by some of the professors but by students as well. The clash between my religious upbringing and formation and my academic theological training was an existentially riveting one for me, and it forced me to think more deeply about these issues than I ever had before.

As I explored these matters more carefully, my conviction was confirmed that classical theology affirmed heaven and hell to be real in a way that resonated with my experience in my little country church. Moreover, given what was at stake in these doctrines, as well as their role in orthodox Christian teaching, it was clear to me that we must come to terms with them in one way or another.

Indeed, I think it is especially incumbent on all who profess orthodox Christianity to remain true to these remarkable doctrines and their far-reaching implications. I find it ironic that contemporary theologians sometimes wax eloquent about the radical nature of Christian theology or the truth of the Christian narrative but become mute or tentative when the issue of heaven is broached. The Christian story is extraordinary, to be sure, but it is radically incomplete and ultimately unsatisfying without a robust doctrine of the afterlife, and one simply cannot seriously affirm Trinity, incarnation, atonement, and resurrection without going on to heartily affirm "the life everlasting."

In my own work as a philosopher of religion, I have been particularly concerned with exploring the rational credentials of these fascinating doctrines and examining the various philosophical issues they involve. I have not only argued that the philosophical challenges they face can be answered but, more positively, I have also contended that these doctrines are powerful resources for addressing some of the most fundamental issues that drive the philosophical enterprise. In particular, I believe these doctrines are most pertinent to such perennial issues as the problem of evil, the nature of personal identity, the foundations of morality, and, ultimately, the very meaning of life.

I have argued this in some detail in a trilogy beginning with my book on hell. I was not planning to write a trilogy at the time, but later reflection led me to see that just as hell poses a distinctive set of interesting issues, so does heaven. So I followed up *Hell: The Logic of Damnation* several years later with *Heaven: The Logic of Eternal Joy*. One of the issues I considered in that book was purgatory, and I devoted a chapter to that doctrine and thought I was done with it. Again, subsequent reflection led me to see that it too poses distinctive issues that deserve fuller exploration, and I was fortunate to receive a research fellowship in the Center for Philosophy of Religion at Notre Dame in 2009–10, where I wrote *Purgatory: The Logic of Total Transformation*.[12] So by a sort of fitting poetic irony, I finished with purgatory where I had started with hell a couple of decades before.

In addition to this trilogy, I have written numerous essays on the afterlife as well as delivered many lectures and sermons on the subject. The present book is my attempt to distill my central thoughts on these issues in a more popular form than my academic books and essays. These issues matter to a far wider audience than professional philosophers and theologians, and I have aimed to communicate the heart of the issues in a way that will be fully accessible to all thoughtful readers who want to think about them more deeply. For those who want to think more deeply still, I urge you to follow up with my trilogy.

Before we proceed, I should say a word about the doctrine of purgatory, a doctrine that many readers will be surprised to see defended by a Protestant philosopher. At this point, I will only say that I am convinced not only that it makes biblical and theological sense but also that it helps us understand heaven, and perhaps hell, much better. Readers can judge whether they agree with me when they have finished the book, but I hope they will not judge before that.

Where to Begin?

As we proceed, an interesting question in its own right is where to begin. Dante's famous masterpiece, the *Divine Comedy*, begins of course with hell, proceeds next to purgatory, and then concludes climactically with heaven. That makes perfect literary and dramatic sense. However, when we think about the matter theologically and philosophically, this may not be the best way to go. For some very profound reasons, hell can be best understood only in light of heaven. And the same is true of purgatory.

The point here is similar to what classic theologians have said about the nature of evil in relation to goodness. The essential point is that evil is not something that exists in its own right in the same way that goodness does. The fundamental reason for this is that God is perfectly good, and everything he created was originally good, even Satan.

Evil, then, must be defined in relation to goodness. As many classic theologians have put it, evil is a privation or a loss of the good. So evil things are good things that have become deformed in some way and thereby have gone bad. In other words, evil is a parasite that can only subsist on things that were originally good by way of corrupting them.

In a similar fashion, hell is to heaven as evil is to goodness. Heaven is the fundamental reality, and we cannot really understand hell unless we understand heaven first, just as we cannot grasp the idea of a fallen world unless we start with a world that is originally good.

As just noted, my own trilogy does not follow this order for reasons already given. I also started with hell and ended,

17

somewhat ironically, with purgatory. But in this book, in which I will deal with all three regions of the afterlife, I shall begin where I think it makes best theological and philosophical sense to begin. When it comes to the things that matter most, heaven is clearly the place to start. So let us now turn our eyes in that direction.

HEAVEN, TRINITY, AND THE
MEANING OF LIFE

"Have you thought of an ending?"

"Yes, several, and they are all dark and unpleasant," said Frodo.

"Oh, that won't do," said Bilbo. "Books ought to have good endings. How would this do: *and they all settled down and lived together happily ever after?*"

"It will do well if it ever comes to that," said Frodo.

"Ah!" said Sam. "And where will they live? That's what I often wonder."

—J. R. R. Tolkien[1]

Any account of the human story that hopes to be credible must be true to the human heart. It must have an honest and realistic grasp of what moves human beings, what drives them to do the things they do. And here, there is a broad consensus among wise observers of the human race. One thing that is absolutely fundamental to human motivation (and apparently hobbit motivation too) is the desire for happiness, and if you fail to grasp the deep significance of this, you cannot possibly understand human nature or human history.

I stress the "deep significance of this" because, unfortunately, for many people the word "happiness" has become tarnished by superficial associations. Indeed, many think the concern with happiness is merely a product of contemporary self-centered consumerist culture.[2] And certainly if happiness is reduced to what money can buy, it is a pretty shallow concept. But the point I am making here is that the quest for happiness has a long-standing legacy that is far richer and more profound than its contemporary commercial caricatures.

A classic statement of the human quest for happiness is by Aristotle, the famous Greek philosopher, in his book *Nicomachean Ethics*. Aristotle opens his book by making the obvious point that every inquiry or undertaking is carried out in the pursuit of some good. The deeper question, Aristotle notes, is whether there is some good that all human beings seek. Aristotle identifies that good as happiness because it is complete in a way other things are not.[3]

To see what he meant, consider your typical college student who spends lots of energy and money to get a good education. We can ask him why he wants that education. The conversation might go something like this.

"I need it to get a good job."

"Why do you want a good job?"

"Because I want to have a family, buy a nice house, drive a fast car, and take vacations in Europe."

"Why do you want a family, a nice house, a fast car, and vacations in Europe?"

"Because if I had all those things I think I'd be happy."

"But why do you want to be happy?"

Long pause . . . incredulous stare . . . he shakes his head and walks away.

The point here obviously is that when we have reached this answer, the question can no longer be sensibly asked. It makes no sense to ask, "Why do you want to be happy?" It is self-evident to any rational person with normal human emotions and feelings. Aristotle, of course, was a pagan philosopher who lived centuries before Christ was born. But it is worth emphasizing that Aristotle's analysis is one that is widely shared not only by classic philosophers but also by Christian thinkers. A notable example is Pascal, the brilliant mathematician and religious thinker of the seventeenth century whom I cited in the introduction. His writings are full of astute observations about the human quest for happiness and the fact that many people seem to be failing badly in that quest. Here is one such example.

> Being unable to cure death, wretchedness and ignorance, men have decided, in order to be happy, not to think about such things. Despite these afflictions man wants to be happy, only wants to be happy, and cannot help wanting to be happy. But how shall he go about it? The best thing would be to make himself immortal, but as he cannot do that, he has decided to stop himself thinking about it.[4]

And now, let's consider a similar observation from John Wesley, the great eighteenth-century theologian and evangelist. Listen to how he addressed the restless seekers of his day: "Do you not still wander to and fro, seeking rest, but finding none? Pursuing happiness, but never overtaking it? And who can blame you for pursuing it? It is the very end of your being. The great Creator made nothing to be miserable, but every creature to be happy in its kind."[5]

Okay, so it is widely agreed that everyone wants to be happy. Indeed, most people don't need a philosophical analysis or an expert's opinion to know this. All they need is even a small dose of self-awareness, and they will see and feel this truth with vivid, and sometimes painful, clarity.

But here is where the broad agreement ends. After this consensus, the questions come charging in. For a start, there is much disagreement on what it takes to make us happy, or what the essential ingredients of happiness are. As Aristotle noted, there are lots of answers to this question. Is it pleasure? Is it power? Is it personal peace of mind? Is it excellence of character? Is it some combination of these, or what?

Is Happiness Even Possible?

These are interesting and important questions, but for now I want to move on to note that there are other questions about happiness that are more unsettling. Perhaps most unnerving of all is this question: Is happiness even achievable? Perhaps none of the answers suggested above, or any other answer, is the correct one. Maybe happiness is some sort of illusion or elusive ideal that no one can really experience. Perhaps at the end of the day it is just a tantalizing temptation, an alluring invitation that we can never actually realize.

Several years ago, a movie came out with the ironic title *Happiness*.[6] I say ironic, because none of the characters were really happy. There were characters chasing happiness in various ways. There were characters pretending to be happy, smiling pleasantly and putting on a good show. There were others trying to convince themselves that they were happy. But the message that came through sharply and disconcertingly was that no one is really happy. Happiness is at best a short-term illusion that will be shattered by hard reality.

Or is it the case that partial happiness is possible, but nothing more? Perhaps we can achieve moments of happiness or approximations of happiness, but that's about it. Perhaps the best "happiness" available consists in the ironic understanding that we can never close the gap between our ideals and the "real world."

And these questions raise other closely related ones. Why do we have such a deeply rooted and pervasive desire for happiness anyway? And is this a blessing or a curse? Recall Pascal's words above, which make it clear that we have no choice in the matter. Not only is it the case that we all want to be happy, but we "cannot help wanting to be happy."

We have a built-in hard drive to desire happiness, but what if that hard drive is a guarantee of frustration, a mechanism that ironically assures our unhappiness because it can never be fully realized? Are we, through no fault of our own, born with an "addiction" for happiness in a universe where it can never be satisfied?

That Elusive Happiness . . . and Love . . .

Now let me venture another observation. Not only do we naturally and perpetually seek happiness; we also seek love. It is perhaps not as self-evident as our desire for happiness, but it is nearly as obvious that normal human beings have a deep yearning to love and to be loved. The countless love songs that pervade our culture, as well as the love poems and songs from centuries past, are eloquent testimony to the human longing for love.

Indeed, we can take this a step further and point out that there is a deep connection between our yearning for love and our desire for happiness. Only if we love and are loved can we be truly and deeply happy. For many people, the essential key to happiness is to find their soul mate, the perfect relationship that they believe will fulfill them and at last provide the happiness they crave.

Unfortunately, this observation only makes the questions about happiness we noted above even more acute. For love seems no less elusive than happiness; perhaps it is even more so. Everyone seems to want it, but lots of people seem to be missing out. Along with all the songs that celebrate love, there are also lots of songs, stories, and movies about broken hearts, frustrated love, unrequited love, looking for love in all the wrong places, and even cynicism about whether real love even exists.

So the question remains whether there is any good reason to think that the happiness gap can or ever will be filled. Are we just stuck with deep and persistent desires for love and happiness that we will take to our graves, but that will never be fully satisfied? And is that the end of the story? If so, the story is a sad one; indeed, it is a tragedy in the classic sense of a story with a painful ending.

Heaven and the Ultimate Romantic Comedy

One of the greatest books ever written is a poetic trilogy about heaven, hell, and purgatory. I refer, of course, to Dante's *Divine Comedy*. The third volume of the trilogy, *Paradiso*, is about heaven, as I noted in the introduction. Accordingly, the book ends on a gloriously happy note, as a comedy in the classic sense must. But the point here is not merely a literary one but also a theological one. Heaven is the end not just of a literary masterpiece but of the entire human drama.

Let us explore this in more detail by turning to the most famous vision of heaven in the Bible, namely, the final three chapters of the book of Revelation. I want to identify seven truths about heaven from these chapters, beginning with this very point that heaven holds out the promise that the human story is destined to come to a wonderful end.

This is suggested with poetic and dramatic force in Revelation 21:6, where we read, "It is done. I am the Alpha and the Omega, the Beginning and the End." Notice immediately that our hopes for the end of the story will be deeply shaped by our view of how the story began. Our view of the Alpha will determine our view of the Omega. This is what gives us hope that the Omega point of human history is one to be eagerly anticipated, not dreaded.

The words "it is done" signal that the human drama spelled out in the pages of Scripture has achieved its proper end. Now the word *end* is a fascinating one that has a double meaning. The common meaning, of course, refers to the conclusion of something, as in the end of a movie. When "The End" appears on the screen, we know the movie is over, the story has been told, and it's time to leave.

But the word *end* also has another meaning that is less common but loaded with deeper significance. The "end" of something in this sense refers to its purpose, its goal, its intended target or outcome. And this is the sense in which God identifies himself as the Alpha and the Omega, the Beginning and the End.

What this means is that God is the Creator of everything, and the ultimate purpose or reason for which everything exists is to be rightly related to God. The implications of this are staggering, to say the least. It means that history is going somewhere and that the human story has an Author and Director who far exceeds what any finite person or group of persons can conceive, plan, or orchestrate. Moreover, he has the power and the wisdom to bring the story to the glorious end for which he created it.

But to truly appreciate why the Author of the human story can bring it to a comic end, we need to understand that there is more to his nature than power and wisdom. Indeed, if we go to the very last line of Dante's *Divine Comedy*, we find a famous description of God that aptly captures what I am talking about. In the final canto of *Paradiso*, Dante has a striking vision of the Trinity, and this moves him to wonder about the mystery of the incarnation, how the divine and human natures were united in Christ. As he ponders these mysteries, his mind is illumined by divine light, and he realizes that his will is completely in tune with love, "the love that moves the sun and the other stars."[7]

Notice that description of God's love. It is "the love that moves the sun and the other stars." This is a striking picture of God as Alpha, the source of all that exists. The ultimate, original reality is not the big bang, it is not matter and energy, nor is it the laws of nature. Behind and before all of these is eternal love.

One of the most extraordinary passages of Scripture is John 17, often referred to as Jesus's "High Priestly Prayer." Here we see the Second Person of the Trinity, the incarnate Son of God, speaking intimately to his Father, the First Person of the Trinity, shortly before he is arrested and offers his life for the salvation of the world. At this crucial moment, we are privileged to listen in as the Eternal Son offers up his prayers for his disciples. And as he anticipates his death, it is amazing to realize that he recalls memories that go all the way back to eternity, before the world was even created. One of the most stunning of these is in verse 24, where he prays that his disciples will be with him to see his glory, which, he says, "you [the Father] have given me because you loved me before the foundation of the world" (NRSV).

Before there was a world or angels or any other created beings over which God ruled as King or Sovereign Lord, God was a Father who had a Son. And the Father and Son and Holy Spirit existed before all worlds in a relationship of perfect love and joyful delight in each other. God did not need a world to love in order for it to be true that "God is love" (1 John 4:16). Rather, the fact that "God is love" is an eternal, fundamental reality.

The church fathers described this eternal relationship of delighted love by using aesthetic images of music and dancing. No doubt C. S. Lewis had these church fathers in mind when he noted "that in Christianity, God is not a static thing—not even a person—but a dynamic, pulsating activity, a life, almost a drama. Almost, if you will not think me irreverent, a kind of dance."[8]

When we let this sink in, we can see why the human drama is a comedy, indeed, a musical comedy that features lots of dancing. Its Author has deep comic sympathies that go all the way back to eternity. Here is another description of God that captures this point, this time from John Wesley. Now keep in mind Wesley's point that we were made for happiness and invariably find ourselves pursuing it. It is no mere coincidence, nor is it an unfortunate curse, that we are constituted this way, for God is "the fountain of happiness, sufficient for all the souls he has made."[9]

The Alpha who created us for happiness is the Omega who is the fountain of happiness. This is the foundational truth that holds out the delicious prospect that the human story is destined for a glorious end that will surpass our wildest imagination.[10]

The Answer to Our Deepest Longings: Three Images

This brings us to a second truth about heaven, namely, that it will answer our deepest longings for happiness and satisfaction. Notice that heaven is described in three images that represent some of our most vivid and familiar desires *and* their fulfillment. Almost everyone knows what it is like to be parched with thirst, to have sharp pangs of hunger, and to feel the powerful yearning of sexual desire. These desires are part of our common experience as human beings, and all of us relish the feeling of having them satisfied.

It is most appealing, then, to read these words of promise from God himself immediately after he identifies himself as the Alpha and the Omega: "To him who is thirsty, I will give to drink without cost from the spring of the water of life" (Rev. 21:6). And in the last chapter of the book the invitation is reiterated: "The Spirit and the bride say, 'Come!' And let him who hears say, 'Come!' Whoever is thirsty, let him come; and whoever wishes, let him take the free gift of the water of life" (Rev. 22:17). Heaven, then, will answer the first of these deeply felt human desires by quenching our thirst for life with the free gift of the water of life. No wonder Wesley described God as "the fountain of happiness, sufficient for all the souls he has made." God's supply of the water of life is infinitely plentiful!

27

A second image of heaven that depicts it as satisfying our quest for happiness and satisfaction is that of a wedding feast. In an earlier chapter, we read, "Blessed are those who are invited to the wedding supper of the Lamb" (Rev. 19:9). Weddings in biblical times were highly festive occasions with ample food and plenty of drinks available. Recall that Jesus's first miracle was turning water into wine at a wedding (John 2). So imagine the joy of sitting down at such a feast when you have not had a meal for a while, and the hunger pangs are dominating your thoughts and feelings.

There is a third picture here—namely, heaven as a wedding— and it is more central to the portrait of heaven than the first two. Indeed, the bridegroom in this wedding is God himself. "I saw the Holy City, the new Jerusalem, coming down out of heaven from God, prepared as a bride beautifully dressed for her husband" (Rev. 21:2; see also 21:9–11). To appreciate this image, think of an engaged couple deeply in love when they finally embrace in marital pleasure on their wedding night.

Now when I say heaven is the satisfaction of our deepest longings and desires for happiness and satisfaction, I do not mean to suggest that those desires will be quenched in the sense that they will be eliminated and we will never feel them again. Rather, our best desires will be ongoing but will not be frustrated as they often are in this life. Rather, they will be fulfilled in an ongoing dynamic fashion, like the newlywed couple on their honeymoon.

Incidentally, a question that is often asked is whether there will be sex in heaven. That's a good question and an altogether natural one to raise, since heaven is a place of perfect happiness, and sex certainly represents one of the deepest and most exciting pleasures of this life. While it is arguable that Scripture does not definitively settle this question, Jesus seems to clearly imply that there will be no sex in heaven when he teaches that there will be no marriage in heaven (Matt. 22:23–32). What we *can* be sure of, however, is that sex is a foretaste of even greater delights in the world to come. The great Christian philosopher Alvin Plantinga puts the point beautifully as follows.

> Sexual eros with its longing and yearning is a sign and fore-shadowing of the yearning for God that will characterize us in our healed and renewed state in heaven; and sexual satisfaction and union, with its transports of ecstasy, is a sign and foreshadowing of the deeper reality of union with God—a union that is at present for the most part obscure to us.[11]

So if sex is in fact absent from heaven, that will not in any way detract from the reality that the fulfillment we experience there will be in every case a step up, not a step down, from the joys and pleasures of this life.[12]

A New Heaven *and* a New Earth

This brings us to a third truth about heaven that further shows why it is the perfect comedic end to the human story. Immediately preceding the verse I quoted above about the Holy City coming down out of heaven, we read this: "Then I saw a new heaven and a new earth, for the first heaven and the first earth had passed away, and there was no longer any sea" (Rev. 21:1). Notice, the Holy City comes down out of heaven to a newly made earth (see again Rev. 21:2, 9–11). Biblical scholars are divided over whether this means that the earth will be entirely new or that this earth will be cleansed and renewed. But what is clear is that heaven will finally be on earth.

It is important to emphasize this to correct a mistaken picture of heaven that is pervasive in popular piety. According to that picture, going to heaven is all about "leaving this old body and this sinful world behind" and flying off to be with God far away from the cares and concerns of planet Earth. But true biblical faith is not about *escape from* the body but rather concerns the *resurrection of* the body. The Apostles' Creed famously expresses that faith in these words: "I believe in the resurrection of the body and the life everlasting." The Christian view of the life everlasting is unequivocally life in a resurrected body.

In popular piety, it is commonly held that we go to heaven when we die and immediately experience the fullness of the eternal life God has in store for us. As N. T. Wright has put it, the popular picture is that going to heaven is a "one-stage postmortem journey."[13] The biblical account of the journey, however, is a bit more complicated. It is more like a flight with a layover than a direct flight. In traditional terms, there is an intermediate stage between death and God's final salvation, during which we await and look forward to the resurrection of our bodies. We will examine this in more detail later, but in most traditional theology, it is held that our souls survive in conscious form in this intermediate stage as we await the resurrection (cf. Rev. 6:9–11).

In fairness to popular piety, many pastors as well as theologians have not always been clear in distinguishing this intermediate stage from the fullness of eternal life that we will enjoy when we are resurrected. Wright has underscored this difference by referring to our future resurrection as "life after life after death"![14] So to apply the metaphor of a flight with a layover, "life after death" is the layover before we reach our final destination. We arrive at our final destination of "life after life after death" not by taking flight from this world and landing in heaven. Rather, our final destination is achieved when heaven comes to this world, when the Holy City, the New Jerusalem comes down to the New Earth.

The main point here is that God's plan of salvation is much larger and more comprehensive than saving human souls, or even human beings. God is saving and redeeming his entire fallen creation. As Paul tells us in Romans, the "whole creation has been groaning as in the pains of childbirth right up to the present time" (Rom. 8:22). And when our redemption is complete, when we are resurrected, the entire created order will also be liberated from sin and redeemed.

If we take Paul's claim about the "whole creation" seriously, I believe—following John Wesley and C. S. Lewis—that we should expect animals to be in heaven. While some may dismiss this out of hand as mere sentimental piety, I would argue that it is an altogether reasonable conviction for those who believe that our world was created by a God of perfect love who cares so deeply for his entire creation that he notices every sparrow that falls (Matt. 10:29).

Lewis argued in particular that pets will be in heaven on the grounds that they have a degree of personality by virtue of their relationship with their masters, and that this identity can be preserved in heaven. "In other words," he wrote, "the man will know his dog: the dog will know its master and, in knowing him, will be itself."[15] Wesley defended a more expansive view of animal immortality, arguing that all animals, not just pets, will be redeemed. Moreover, he dared to speculate that in the world to come, animals might even be given enhanced powers of understanding that would make them capable of a relationship with God.[16]

Perhaps this is part of what is involved in the fulfillment of that extraordinary prophecy of a day to come when the earth will be full of the knowledge of the Lord, and the wolf will lie down in peace with the lamb (Isa. 11:6–9). It is also worth noting that the account of heavenly worship in Revelation describes four creatures who join in praising God, three of which are like a lion, an ox, and an eagle (Rev. 4:6–8). Immediately after this, we are told that the twenty-four elders sing these words in praise to God: "You are worthy, our Lord and God, to receive glory and honor and power, for you created all things, and by your will they were created and have their being" (Rev. 4:11). The God who created "all things" is fittingly praised, it seems, by all his creatures.[17]

31

To reiterate the main point, we cannot have a good theology of salvation if we do not begin with a good theology of creation. This whole world is God's creation, just as our bodies are his creation that he pronounced to be good. God is not consigning our bodies to the dustbin and saving only our souls. "Ashes to ashes, dust to dust" is not the last word on our bodies. No! And the fact that he is redeeming our bodies is emblematic of his larger goal of saving his good but fallen creation in its entirety.

That is one reason why it is crucial to emphasize that our salvation was achieved by Jesus taking on a full human nature, living a life of perfect obedience to the Father in this world, and feeling real pain and anguish in a real human body and soul when he died for us. And that is why it is essential that his resurrection was a bodily one that left the tomb empty on Easter morning. The resurrection of Jesus is God's promise to us that we too shall be resurrected and have a body like Jesus's risen body.

Christ's resurrection is the beginning of the new creation. But there is unfinished business. The full impact of Easter is yet to be seen and felt. When our bodies are raised and heaven comes to a renewed earth, God will have finished the work he began when he raised Jesus from the dead. When heaven comes to earth, when the prayer that Jesus taught us to pray—"Your kingdom come, your will be done, on earth as it is in heaven"—is fully answered, then the work of Easter will be done.

The Death of Death

This brings us to a fourth truth about heaven that is packed with comic significance, and indeed, it is one of the most poignantly beautiful promises in the Bible. "He will wipe every tear from their eyes. There will be no more death or mourning or crying or pain, for the old order of things has passed away" (Rev. 21:4). Notice this text recognizes that mourning and tears are an altogether natural and appropriate part of a world filled with death and pain. And if this were the last word, the human drama would be a tragedy. Christians should not be in denial about the painful realities of our world. There is a time to weep, and indeed, those times come all too often and inevitably in this life. But when heaven comes to earth in all its fullness, the time for weeping will be over. Death, crying, and pain will be no more. They are part of the "old order of things" that will have passed away. Life, laughter, and pleasure will be the last word rather than death, crying, and pain. (We will explore this more fully in a later chapter.)

The Reunion of Truth, Beauty, and Goodness

A fifth truth about heaven is that it will represent the perfect unity of truth, beauty, and goodness. According to the Christian vision of reality, these three great ideals are unified; they are aspects of an integrated whole. By contrast, one of the hallmarks of the modern/postmodern period of history is the shattering and fragmentation of this unity. Indeed, the philosopher Susan Nieman has suggested that the quest to find the unity between these three great ideals is at the heart of the philosophical enterprise. She writes, "The drive to metaphysics is a drive to find a real order behind the apparent one, in which all the things we long for—the good and the true and the beautiful—will be connected and revealed."[18] Many philosophers have despaired of ever finding this unity and have reconciled themselves to the harsh conclusion that the connection between truth, beauty, and goodness is irreparably broken.

We can also see the fractured remains of this previous unity in much of pop culture. Stories and songs that are "honest" and "real" are often dark and painful. In other words, the unvarnished truth is not beautiful, nor is it good. In this situation, many feel we are faced with the painful choice of embracing a harsh reality or a beautiful fantasy or illusion. Indeed, a common expression conveys the inevitability of this fragmentation. How often have all of us heard someone say with respect to some wonderful prospect that it is "just too good to be true"?

In fact, this is what many people think about heaven. I recall a conversation from several years ago with one of my friends and his wife, both of whom are atheists. As we were talking about heaven, she exclaimed, "It is such a beautiful idea, but I just can't believe it is true."

As we read the description of heaven in the book of Revelation, we might find our hearts longing for such a place but wondering if it is nothing more than a wonderful fantasy. The physical description of heaven is famous for its depiction of stunning beauty. In addition to streets of gold, it is said that it "shone with the glory of God, and its brilliance was like that of a very precious jewel, like a jasper, clear as crystal" (Rev. 21:11). But even more appealing is the assurance that heaven is perfectly good. Not only are death and mourning eliminated, but "nothing impure will ever enter it" (Rev. 21:27; cf. also 22:14–15).

In view of our fear that it's just too good to be true, it is noteworthy to read, "He who was seated on the throne said, 'I am making everything new!' Then he said, 'Write this down, for these words are trustworthy and true'" (Rev. 21:5; cf. 22:6). God himself addresses us from his throne to assure us that perfect beauty and goodness will connect with truth when he makes all things new, never again to be broken apart.

Celebrating the Best of Human Culture

A sixth truth is that heaven will preserve and celebrate the best of human culture. We see this indicated in the following: "The glory and honor of the nations will be brought into [the city]" (Rev. 21:26). Earlier in the book, we learn that heaven will include people "from every nation, tribe, people and language"

(Rev. 7:9; cf. 5:9). This suggests that part of the fascination and delight of heaven will be composed of enjoying the multifaceted products of human creativity represented by every nation, tribe, and language under the sun.

Recall that God gave humans what is called his "cultural mandate" in the very beginning when he commanded them to "fill the earth and subdue it" (Gen. 1:28). This means we are not only permitted but commanded to explore and develop the potentialities and possibilities that God built into the earth by design when he created it. Indeed, our acts of creativity expand upon and elaborate God's creation, so when we create, we are in a sense cocreating with him.

Now the human record on this score is obviously mixed. We can point with pride to the music of Bach, the fiction of Tolkien, the architecture of Westminster Abbey, the Pyramids, and the Taj Mahal, but we must recoil in shame at weapons of mass destruction, implements of torture, and the pollution that has marred the beauty of nature.

Since God is renewing and redeeming his creation, and heaven is the climax of that redemption, there is every reason to believe that our cultural mandate will remain in effect in the new creation. Not only will the best of human culture be preserved and celebrated for our ongoing enjoyment, but also new works will be created, including no doubt countless new forms of creativity we have yet to imagine. No doubt the most moving pieces of music, the most beautiful paintings and poems, the most magnificent buildings, the most profound scientific discoveries, the most fascinating novels, plays, movies, and so on have yet to be conceived and produced.

The Climax: At Home with God!

Seventh and finally, heaven is being at home with God. This is not only the climactic truth about heaven; it is also the central reality that makes heaven the satisfaction of our deepest longings and aspirations. After the account of the Holy City coming down from heaven as a bride beautifully dressed for her husband, we read, "And I heard a loud voice from the throne saying, 'Now the dwelling of God is with men and he will live with them. They will be his people, and God himself will be with them and be their God'" (Rev. 21:3).

The modest little preposition "with," which appears three times in this verse, is actually one of the most beautiful and suggestive words in human language. In particular, it often signals the profound truth that one is not alone. Indeed, the word is used to convey everything from mere physical presence to relationships of a deeper sort, including sexual intimacy. And the most wonderful and fulfilling of all relationships is a relationship with God. Notice: "God himself will be with them and be their God."

And when God is with us, when he lives with us, we will feel at home in this world in a way we never have before. For that was God's plan from the beginning, as pictured in the garden of Eden. He wanted to live with us in a close, loving relationship, one in which we would feel complete joy and peace in his presence. While even now we can enjoy a personal relationship with God, we must also recognize that we are still living in a fallen world that is "groaning for redemption." As such, we are not fully at home in this world in the way God originally intended us to be. Heaven is our true home, but we are not there yet, and we should not pretend that we are. This world is still marred by sin, death, and mourning, all of which cause those tears that God promises to wipe away.

We already have, of course, a powerful foreshadowing of what it will be like for God to live with us in the life of Christ when he walked on earth. Recall that one of the names that Isaiah the prophet gave the promised Messiah was Immanuel, which means "God with us" (Isa. 7:14; cf. Matt. 1:23). This extraordinary truth is also conveyed by John, who named Jesus the Word who was with God in the beginning and who was God (John 1:1). And in one of the most famous descriptions of the incarnation, he went on to say, "The Word became flesh and made his dwelling among us" (John 1:14). Notice, the Word was "with" God, and he came to dwell among (with) us.

This profound description of the incarnation is echoed in Revelation. Indeed, the same verb that is used in John 1:14 to describe Jesus "dwelling" among us is also used in Revelation 21:3. God will be with us; he himself will live with us and be our God. Only a few people had the extraordinary experience of being with Jesus when he walked this earth, but heaven holds out the promise that all who trust him for salvation will one day live with God on this earth in perfect intimacy.

Indeed, Revelation goes on to tell us something even more astounding, namely, that the inhabitants of the Holy City "will see [God's] face, and his name will be on their foreheads" (Rev. 22:4). This is astounding, because in the Old Testament, when Moses asked to see God's glory, God allowed him to see his "back" but said, "You cannot see my face, for no one may see me and live" (Exod. 33:20). So what was denied one of the greatest of Old Testament saints will be the extraordinary privilege of all the redeemed in heaven.

The promise that we shall see the face of God is the basis for one of the most famous ideas about heaven in classical theology, namely, the "beatific vision." The word *beatific* means "blissfully happy," so the idea here is that seeing the face of God will elicit supreme happiness and joy from all who see it. Indeed, so wonderful is the beatific vision that some classical theologians suggest that it is not only the very essence of heaven but pretty much the whole of it. In this view, heaven is a sort of timeless bliss that results from being so absorbed in the vision of God that we tend to lose any awareness of anything else. So given this view, the other features of heaven will add little to our joy and happiness. Our resurrected bodies, the new earth, relationships with other persons, creative and cultural activities, and so on will pale into insignificance in light of the beatific vision.[19]

By contrast, New Testament scholar Ben Witherington takes Scripture to suggest that the beatific vision is an experience that will occur in human community. Commenting on Revelation 21:3, he notes that "humanity will finally see God and his glorious presence and live. This has traditionally been called the beatific vision, but it happens in the midst of the people of God, not as an isolated, mystical experience."[20]

This is a more natural way to understand the beatific vision from the standpoint of a strong creation theology. Randy Alcorn, who has made the case at length for a fully physical heaven, complete with all the essential features of any good society, contends that it is a grave error to divorce our experience of God from our experience of the things that give us joy in this life.

> It [the grave error] sees the material realm and other people as God's competitors rather than as instruments that communicate his love and character. It fails to recognize that because God is the ultimate source of joy, and all secondary joys emanate from him, to love secondary joys on earth *can be*—and in heaven *always will be*—to love God, their source.[21]

So here is a paradox; indeed, we can call it the love paradox. If we love God most of all, we are thereby inspired to love other things more deeply and truly than we would if we loved them more than we love God.[22] To see God's face in heaven will not mean that our interest in other people and other created things will diminish or even that we will love them less. Rather, it means we will see God clearly in all his good gifts, and we will love and enjoy them *even more* as a result.

Since God's entire creation reflects his glory, we get some preliminary glimpses of this aspect of heaven even in this life. Consider the joy and beauty that sometimes overwhelm us as we watch the sun set over the ocean or find ourselves entranced as we view a great work of art or listen to a stirring piece of music. Or consider the profound delight and gratitude we feel as we gaze into the eyes of someone we love, whether a spouse, a child, or a grandchild. In these sorts of experiences, Alvin Plantinga notes, "there is a kind of yearning, something perhaps a little like nostalgia, or perhaps homesickness, a longing for we know not what."[23]

The homesickness is for heaven, the longing we feel is to be fully at home with God, and the nostalgia is for Eden. All these profound yearnings will be fulfilled when we see God with stunning clarity everywhere we look and enjoy the pleasure of his intimate presence with us.

It is worth underscoring in this connection that the description of the Holy City we have been examining prominently includes images of Eden.[24] In particular, we are told that the river of the water of life flows down the middle of the main street and that on either side of the river stands the tree of life bearing fruit every month (Rev. 22:1–2). In the early chapters of Genesis, of course, Adam and Eve were barred from eating from the tree of life after sinning against God and breaking fellowship with him. But now that heaven has come to earth, and the curse is no more, there is free access to the tree of life and the promise that its leaves will provide healing for the nations.

This is the life for which we were created, to be fully at home with God in the world he created for us to enjoy and to see his face reflecting his love and glory everywhere we look. With Eden thus restored, the tragic turn taken by the human drama in Genesis has been altogether overcome. Indeed, the human drama comes to the perfect comic end, one of unsurpassable beauty and goodness.

A Misguided Spirituality, an Impoverished View of Heaven

Several years ago a movie came out entitled *Michael*, in which John Travolta plays the starring role of an angel who is permitted one more visit to earth before he must go to heaven forever.[25] The implicit message is that heaven is an ethereal, cold, blood-less, and boring place, whereas earth with its carnal pleasures is where the real joy and vitality are to be found. To be deprived of earth and consigned to heaven thus appears to be more like an eternal death sentence than an eternal reward.

What we have seen from the sketch above is that it is a pro-found mistake to set heaven over against earth in that way. To aspire to heaven does not require turning our backs on earth with all its pleasures. Rather, it is about longing for God's will to be done on earth as it is in heaven. God's final end is ac-complished not by undoing or destroying his originally good creation but by redeeming and renewing it. So the notion that we must choose between heaven and earth is simply a false di-lemma. To choose heaven is to choose earth at its best, as God ultimately intends it to be.

Lying at the root of this false dilemma is often a deeply mis-guided, though often sincere, notion of spirituality. For many Christians, the thought that heaven will be a physical place and that it will include bodily, cultural, and social pleasures seems unworthy of God. Persons who are truly spiritual, it is thought, should be above such concerns.

Here it is important to distinguish two senses of *spiritual* that are easily and often confused. First, that which is spiritual can refer simply to anything that is nonmaterial. Thus souls, angels, and God are examples of things that are spiritual in this sense, whereas bodies, basketballs, and blueberries are not. But second, the word *spiritual* can also mean anything that is in ac-cord with God's will, anything that honors and glorifies him.[26]

Now this is what is important to see. Not everything that is spiritual in the first sense is spiritual in the second. Demons and fallen angels, for instance, are "spiritual" in the first sense but not the second. Just because something is not material does not make it good or assure that it honors and glorifies God.

Moreover, there are things that are not spiritual in the first sense that are spiritual in the second. Take eating, for instance, an activity that at one level can be viewed as purely physical or biological and one we share with dogs, cows, sharks, and mice. For Christians, however, eating should be a deeply spiritual matter. Recall Paul's words: "So whether you eat or drink or whatever you do, do it all for the glory of God" (1 Cor. 10:31). Notice, we are to do it all for the glory of God. In other words, everything about our lives should be spiritual.

I have always been fascinated in this regard by a passage in the Old Testament. In Exodus 24, after the giving of the Ten Commandments, God confirms his covenant with Moses and the Israelites. On this occasion, God calls seventy of the Israelite elders along with Moses, his brother, Aaron, and a couple of other men to worship on Mount Sinai. Here is the passage I find fascinating. "Moses and Aaron, Nadab and Abihu, and the seventy elders of Israel went up and saw the God of Israel. Under his feet was something like a pavement made of sapphire, clear as the sky itself" (Exod. 24:9–10).

This must have been an awesome experience, a spiritual encounter of extraordinary power. And how do you think they reacted? Would you expect that they would be on their faces in awe, perhaps even terror in the presence of the Holy One of Israel? Well, here is the next verse: "But God did not raise his hand against these leaders of the Israelites; they saw God, and they ate and drank." Did you get that? "They saw God, and they ate and drank"! I would guess these men never looked at a meal the same way again!

Now if we are to do all things for the glory of God, does this mean we must do everything with a somber mind-set and never laugh and have fun? Not at all! Indeed, it is just the opposite. To eat to the glory of God is to eat with a sense of gratitude and joy; it is to recognize that our food is a gift of God. Gratitude is by definition a happy state of mind. Recognizing God as the source of all good things enhances our joy; it does not diminish it.

It is crucial not only for our understanding of heaven but also for our Christian life as a whole that we learn to resist the misguided notion of spirituality that sets the material world in opposition to God. To fall into this misguided notion of spirituality is, in effect, to hand over God's good world to Satan and to give the impression that he invented physical beauty, fun, laughter, pleasure, and so on. And to give Satan the credit for the material world results in a view of spirituality that is thin, shriveled, and fragmented and a view of heaven that is correspondingly impoverished.

Can You Believe It? A Dancing God?

One of the most strident critics of the doctrine of heaven is, not surprisingly, one of the most hostile opponents of Christianity in the history of Western thought. I refer to Friedrich Nietzsche, my favorite atheist. Nietzsche was the son of a pastor. His father died when Nietzsche was just five years old, which left a profound and lasting mark on him.

The last book he wrote before he went insane was *The Antichrist*, his most bitter attack on the faith he rejected as an adolescent. In that book he claims that the "most contemptible of all unrealisable promises" generated by the Christian gospel is "the *impudent* doctrine of personal immortality."[27] The notion that ordinary people like first-century fishermen could aspire to immortality was laughable to Nietzsche, and he pulled no punches in pouring out his scorn on the idea.

Before saying where I think Nietzsche got things utterly and profoundly wrong, it is worth noting that some of his criticisms were on target. Indeed, it appears that many of the Christians with whom he was most familiar had a badly deficient creation theology. Many of them seemed to advocate the misguided sort of spirituality we examined above. They seemed to be people who disdained the body as well as the material world and professed to care only for the life to come.

It was Nietzsche's belief that many people who professed such things did not really feel that way but pretended to do so because they thought it was "spiritual" to do so. The honest person, he contended, valued the body, even when he pretended not to. Nietzsche's "gospel" was a call to forthrightly love the body and the earth and all that they offer us. "A new pride my ego taught me, and this I teach men: no longer to bury one's head in the sand of heavenly beings, but to bear it freely, an earthly head, which creates a meaning for the earth."[28]

Christians who devalue the body and trivialize this earth had their heads in the sand in his view and were neither honest nor realistic. While they professed values that sounded lofty and high minded, in Nietzsche's view, they were in fact deluded and unhealthy.

Despite his own poor health and other personal struggles, Nietzsche strongly affirmed the goodness of this life. Indeed, one of the things that struck me several years ago in reading through one of his most famous books, *Thus Spake Zarathustra*, is how often he praises dancing and expresses his own desire to dance. In one of these passages, he even states the sort of God he would believe in: "I would believe only in a god who could dance. And when I saw my devil I found him serious, thorough, profound, and solemn: it was the spirit of gravity—through him all things fall."[29]

On these points I must agree with Nietzsche. Christians who despise the body and devalue the world of physical creation distort and diminish their own faith, including the doctrine of heaven. And I wish Nietzsche had understood that Christians of all people have the most reason to dance, because God is the God of the dance. Randy Alcorn sums up the point nicely: "If you believe Satan invented dancing or that dancing is inherently sinful, you give Satan too much credit and God too little."[30]

And yet Nietzsche went wrong at a more profound level that kept him from seeing a God who could dance. What blinded Nietzsche to the dancing God was that he could not believe that love of the kind Christianity teaches is real. In one of the most revealing passages in all his works, he offers his analysis of what he calls "that most brilliant stroke of Christianity: God's sacrifice of himself for man." Here is Nietzsche's account: "God makes himself the ransom for what could not otherwise be ransomed; God alone has power to absolve us of a debt we can no longer discharge; the creditor offers himself as a sacrifice for his debtor out of sheer love (can you believe it?), out of love for his debtor."[31]

Of course, Christians themselves have always been staggered by the astounding truth at the heart of the gospel: that God loves us so much that he gave his Son to die for our salvation. Think, for instance, of Isaac Watts's famous hymn "When I Survey the Wondrous Cross" and the amazement he expresses that God could love us so much.

Nietzsche clearly felt what a shocking claim it is that God would die on a cross. Earlier in the same book, he asks, "What could equal in debilitating narcotic power the symbol of the 'holy cross,' the ghastly paradox of a crucified god, the unspeakably cruel mystery of God's self-crucifixion for the benefit of mankind?"[32] But while Nietzsche felt the shock, he did not respond with gratitude and worship. Rather, he was simply incredulous. "Can you believe it?" he asks, making clear that for him it is inconceivable that such love could actually exist.

A Tale of Two Lambs

According to the Christian story, such love is an eternal, primordial reality, as we saw above. One of the most beautiful pictures of this love is conveyed in the New Testament image of Jesus as the perfect lamb who was sacrificed for our sins (John 1:35–36;

Rev. 5:6–12). Indeed, there are texts that suggest that Jesus as the Lamb of God was in some sense slain before the world was ever created (Rev. 13:8; 1 Pet. 1:18–21). That is to say, God loves us with an eternal love and was already prepared to pay the price for our salvation before he ever created the world.

Nietzsche had an altogether different view of ultimate, primordial reality. In his vision of things, the bottom-line reality is what he called "the will to power," which is the natural tendency of the strong to dominate the weak. The powerful automatically exercise their power over the powerless, and as Nietzsche saw it, this is not only natural; it is inevitable. The will to power is the true engine that drives the world, the real dynamic that courses through the world and makes it go as it does. In one of his more memorable expressions of this view, he puts it like this:

> There is nothing very odd about lambs disliking birds of prey, but that is no reason for holding it against large birds of prey that they carry off lambs. . . . To expect that strength will not manifest itself as strength, as the desire to overcome, to appropriate, to have enemies, obstacles, and triumphs, is every bit as absurd as to expect that weakness will manifest itself as strength.[33]

Indeed, Nietzsche was so skeptical of the idea that a being who was strong might not dominate the weak that he ridiculed as mere superstition the notion that "it is within the discretion of the strong to be weak, of the bird of prey to be a lamb."[34]

And yet that is exactly what Christianity says God did when his Son became the lamb who was sacrificed for our sins. The one who holds all power revealed himself most clearly not in domination but in becoming a lamb and submitting to death on the cross before rising again.

Notice, the lamb who was slain is at the center of the throne in the book of Revelation (Rev. 5:6; 7:17). The lamb is not weak by nature but rather is supremely powerful. His "weakness" in dying for our sins was not imposed on him by someone stronger than him but was, rather, an expression of the power of perfect love. Jesus was very clear that no one had the power to take his life from him but that he laid it down in love to his Father. "No one takes it from me, but I lay it down of my own accord. I have authority to lay it down and authority to take it up again. This command I received from my Father" (John 10:18).

Nietzsche simply could not conceive of love like this really existing, and this was the deepest reason he found the idea of heaven preposterous. And this, I want to emphasize, is *the* watershed issue. Is Dante right that love moves the stars, or is Nietzsche right that the will to power makes the world go round? Do the strong inevitably dominate the weak like those birds of prey that carry off lambs, or is ultimate truth both more surprising and more beautiful than we could ever have guessed?

Nietzsche's Alpha was the will to power, so he could not imagine an Omega where perfect love is the order of the day. But if the Trinity is the Alpha and the Omega, then heaven makes perfect sense. If the Trinity is bedrock reality, then love is the very heart of the meaning of life. And when perfect love achieves its ends, we may hope to find the perfect happiness we crave, the perfect comic end of the cosmic drama.

2

CONSOLATION MEASURES
WHEN THE DREAM HAS DIED

The last act is bloody, however fine the rest of the play.
They throw earth over your head and it is finished forever.

—Pascal[1]

Dreams die hard. The more wonderful a dream is, the more
it captures our heart, the more it fires our imagination,
and the more difficult it is to give it up.

As we have seen, heaven represents the ultimate dream, the
perfect comic ending to the human story, and it is hard to see
how anyone who has heard of it could not at least hope it is
true. Even those who do not believe in it often confess that it
is a deeply moving and beautiful idea and express regret that
they cannot believe in it. When faced with the difficult choice
between beauty and what they believe to be true, they reluctantly
give up beauty and opt for what they take to be the hard truth.

Moreover, the idea of heaven has deeply shaped Western culture for most of two thousand years. It has been celebrated in great poetry, classic paintings, and other art forms. Even today it often comes up as the subject of movies and popular songs. Recent examples are Los Lonely Boys' hit song "Heaven," which was played on both pop and country stations, as well as MercyMe's crossover hit, "I Can Only Imagine." Heaven is in our cultural blood, it is in our emotional DNA, and there is no getting around it.

To surrender the hope of heaven is no small matter. Indeed, it requires not only an enormous intellectual shift but also a profound adjustment of our emotions and outlook on the future. To give up the hope of heaven requires us to radically scale down the level of happiness we can hope to attain and to live with much smaller dreams.

To get a sense of this, let us consider a vision of reality and of the end of the cosmic drama that does not include heaven. This comes from Bertrand Russell, one of the most famous philosophers of the twentieth century, and it depicts the human story from the vantage point of atheism. It is one of the most frequently quoted passages in recent philosophy because of the graphically memorable way he pictures the human condition if we are the sole authors, producers, and directors of the human drama. It illustrates again that our view of the Alpha will determine our view of the Omega.

That man is the product of causes which had no prevision of the end they were achieving; that his origin, his growth, his hopes and fears, his loves and his beliefs, are but the outcome of accidental collocations of atoms; that no fire, no heroism, no intensity of thought and feeling, can preserve an individual life beyond the grave; that all the labor of the ages, all the devotion, all the inspiration, all the noonday brightness of human genius, are destined to extinction in the vast death of the solar system, and that the whole temple of man's achievement must inevitably be buried beneath the debris of a universe in ruins—all these things, if not quite beyond dispute, are yet so nearly certain that no philosophy which rejects them can hope to stand. Only within the scaffolding of these truths, only on the firm foundation of unyielding despair, can the soul's habitation henceforth be safely built.[2]

Notice in the first place that Russell's "alpha" is a blind creator with no end in mind. Indeed, the "accidental collocations of atoms" that he cites have no mind or intentions. So nothing or no one intended for us to be here, and there was no goal or purpose in our coming into existence. No end, no "omega" was previsioned for the human story. However, Russell does envision an end of the human story, and it is rather gloomy to say the least. It is an end in the sense of a *termination*, not in the deeper sense of a *destination* or purpose achieved. The end will come when the energy in the universe runs down, and the universe comes to utter ruin as it eventually disintegrates and dissipates.

Radically Different Visions

Notice how thoroughly and sharply this vision contrasts with the vision of heaven in Revelation. Whereas heaven represents the satisfaction of our deepest longings for happiness and satisfaction, Russell leaves us with "the firm foundation of unyielding despair." Whereas heaven promises the redemption of the entire created order, Russell's vision anticipates a universe in ruins. Whereas heaven promises the end of death, mourning, and tears, this vision ends with the vast death of the solar system, shutting down once and for all any prospect of individual survival beyond the grave. Whereas heaven promises the preservation and perfection of the best of human culture, Russell's vision resigns "the whole temple of man's achievement" to extinction and burial "beneath the debris of a universe in ruins." Whereas heaven promises a convergence of truth, beauty, and goodness, for Russell the "scaffolding of truth" that is "so nearly certain" that no one can rationally reject it utterly dashes any such hope. And whereas heaven promises that we will be with God on a restored earth that will be fully home for us, for Russell the universe ends in a fashion that is utterly hostile and alien to human beings.

The contrast between these two visions could hardly be greater. Whereas one ends tragically, the other ends as a glorious comedy. Whereas one is driven by blind accident, the other is intelligently and lovingly directed to a "previsioned" end that is wondrously good. One represents the fulfillment of our deepest and most cherished dreams, and the other the devastating death of those dreams.

Again, dreams die hard. Even when people deny the reality of heaven and give up belief in it, they still pursue it in other ways. The yearning for heaven is just too deeply rooted to simply disappear. Consider these revealing words from Bertrand Russell himself, in a letter he wrote: "The centre of me is always and eternally a terrible pain . . . a searching for something beyond what the world contains, something transfigured and infinite. The beatific vision—God. I do not find it, I do not think it is to be found—but the love of it is my life. . . . It is the actual spring of life within me."[3]

So Russell here concedes that the quest for heaven continues despite the denial that it can ever be found. In this chapter I want to examine some of the ways philosophers have attempted to compensate for losing the dream of heaven. In particular, I will examine some substitutes for heaven that have been constructed to fill the gaping hole that is left in our hearts when heaven is denied. I will also consider moves that are made to provide consolation for the loss of meaning that follows when the dream of heaven has died.

An Uninspiring Call to Worship

So let us begin with Russell's own substitute version of heaven. The title of the essay from which the quote above comes is "A Free Man's Worship." Strikingly, Russell's essay is full of religious imagery and language as he spells out his account of "worship" for atheists. His aim is to explain how our highest human ideals can be maintained in a world that is hostile to them. This requires a twofold wisdom on our part.

First, we must come to terms with the fact that the world was not made to satisfy our aspirations, and we must resign ourselves to this reality. True wisdom is coming to understand that "the world was not made for us, and that however beautiful may be the things we crave, Fate may nevertheless forbid them."[4] The world of fact, the world of physics and natural law, marches on irresistibly to an end that will completely crush our dreams, and we are utterly powerless to stop it.

Now in the face of this harsh reality, it is tempting to give up our ideals and simply go with the flow and worship power. (Russell cites Nietzsche as someone who takes this line.) However, Russell urges us to resist this temptation, and this brings us to the second component of the twofold wisdom he recommends. In addition to resigning ourselves to the fact that the world was not made for us and will crush our dreams, we must nevertheless continue to worship our ideals. Here is Russell's call to worship and his substitute for heaven.

> Let us preserve our respect for truth, beauty, for the ideal of perfection which life does not permit us to attain, though none of these things meet with the approval of the unconscious universe. If power is bad, as it seems to be, let us reject it from our hearts. In this lies man's true freedom: in determination to worship only the God created by our own love of the good, to respect only the heaven which inspires the insight of our best moments.[5]

Notice the call to preserve respect for ideals "which life does not permit us to attain" and to worship a "God" of our own creation, namely, our own love of the good. And what is his idea of heaven? Well, heaven is what inspires the insight we have in our best moments.

Now this is a terribly diminished account of God and of heaven, and it doesn't take a lot of reflection to see that even this shriveled version of heaven doesn't fare too well in light of Russell's larger picture of reality. Recall his comment above that all our hopes, loves, and beliefs "are but the outcome of accidental collocations of atoms." If all our beliefs are produced by random combinations of atoms, is there any reason to prefer the ideals Russell urges us to honor instead of worshiping power? Is there any compelling reason why we *should* give more respect to beauty and perfection than to force and destruction? This question is even more urgent if force and destruction will "win" at the end of the day when the laws of nature eventually cause the "vast death of the solar system."

It is important to note that at this point in his career, Russell believed in objective moral values despite his atheism. He thought that the great ideals of truth, beauty, and perfection were values that all rational persons *should* respect and attempt to honor. Later, however, Russell came to the conclusion that there is no good reason to believe these values are objectively true and hold for all persons. Rather, he came to believe that his moral convictions were only subjective and that, strictly speaking, there is no such thing as truth or knowledge when it comes to morality. As he bluntly put it, "Outside human desires, there is no moral standard."[6]

He realized, moreover, that in giving up objective morality, he gave up any claim that others *should* accept his moral views. He conceded that he was doing nothing more than stating his personal preferences when he put forward his moral views. The most he could do was to offer his vision of the good life and hope that as many as possible would share his perspective.

So what does he recommend in this regard? Here is his view in a nutshell: "*The good life is one inspired by love and guided by knowledge.*"[7] A little later in his essay, Russell spells out a bit more what his ideal world would look like. "In a perfect world, every sentient being would be to every other the object of the fullest love, compounded by delight, benevolence, and understanding inextricably blended."[8]

Now it is striking that his "perfect world" looks a lot like heaven. It is a world in which love and delight characterize all relationships. Russell goes on, however, to admit that his ideal could not be achieved in the actual world. The best we can do is approximate it in a way that will still fall far short of perfection.

So Russell's substitute for heaven is paltry indeed when carefully examined. It is only an ideal that reflects nothing more than Russell's personal preferences and desires, but one we have no reason to hope will ever be realized. Russell can urge that we refuse to worship power and worship instead what he believes are our best ideals. He can urge us to create as far as humanly possible a society of love and knowledge, a world that approximates his "perfect world."

However, he gives us no reason to believe that love is a fundamental reality or that it will prevail over injustice and power in the end. To the contrary, the unbreakable laws of nature will roll on inexorably until everything that love ever built or inspired has been destroyed—every home, every relationship, every poem, every song, every smile, and every kiss. He can urge that love should be honored over power, but he has precious little to say to those who believe that might makes right and that "knowledge" is whatever those in power say it is.

Such a "heaven" is at best an empty shadow of the Christian account of heaven and offers us very little even by way of inspiration. Russell's call to worship rings hollow indeed.

Rolling Stones That Give No Satisfaction

Next, let us consider another salvage operation to give meaning to our lives without heaven. This comes from Richard Taylor, who takes the famous myth of Sisyphus as his starting point. Sisyphus, recall, was the mythical character condemned by the gods to push a large stone up a hill, which then rolled back down to the bottom, only to be pushed up again, and again, forever.

At first glance this does not seem to be a very promising point of departure for someone who wants to defend the meaning of life. Indeed, Sisyphus seems to be the very epitome of a meaningless existence, the poster child for futility. What could be more absurd than being consigned to a monotonous existence of repeating the same boring task over and over again, only to see it undone every time you did it?

Taylor, however, sees Sisyphus as an illuminating image of the human situation, for we pursue goals that have only temporal significance and then move on to other goals. The main difference between us and Sisyphus is that whereas he continues to push the stone up the hill forever, we pass the task on to our children. They then pick up where we left off and continue in our steps. Civilizations are built and destroyed, but new ones are built on the rubble of earlier ones. We just keep picking up the stones and building afresh, and the beat goes on. We are all Sisyphus, and we are all rolling stones.

Does this show that our lives are meaningless? Taylor thinks not, and he offers a variation on the Sisyphus story that he thinks makes that famous case even more like the human condition. Imagine, he suggests, that the gods have mercy on Sisyphus by putting a substance in his veins that causes him to have an obsession with rolling stones. As a result of this, he does not find it monotonous to roll the stone up the hill continually, nor does it frustrate him when it rolls right back down. To the contrary, it brings him delight because it enables him to continue with his obsession of rolling the stone up the hill. Indeed, Taylor suggests that this scenario would actually provide Sisyphus with heavenly bliss, for he could go on forever indulging his never-ending desire to roll stones.

Moreover, he thinks this shows why our lives have a meaning that is actually superior to anything heaven can offer. For the human situation is very much like the scenario where the gods implant the substance in Sisyphus's veins that gives him his obsession with rolling stones. All of us are born, Taylor thinks, with an instinctive will to live. There are tasks to be done, and we have a natural desire to do them. Our parents had the same natural compulsion and so will our children, and their children, and so on. The drug is in our veins, so to speak, and it drives us to carry on the human project.

If this is not enough for us and we find this depressing, well, the problem is that we are seeking a meaning to our lives that simply does not exist. Taylor urges us to keep this in mind and then concludes his essay with this extraordinary claim: "The meaning of life is from within us, it is not bestowed from without, and it far exceeds in both its beauty and its permanence any heaven of which men have ever dreamed or yearned for."[9]

I say this is an extraordinary claim, and really, I find it one of the most implausible claims I have ever read—certainly about heaven. As Taylor sees it, the meaning of our lives is entirely a matter of whatever satisfaction we experience from doing the tasks we naturally find ourselves disposed to do. Why we have the compulsion to pursue the tasks we do, or whether there is any ultimate point to it all, is apparently irrelevant. Indeed, the most meaningful life is apparently one that never raises these questions. Socrates famously said that the unexamined life is not worth living. Taylor apparently thinks the unexamined life of rolling stones is as good as it gets.

At one level, the simplicity of this view is rather appealing. Unfortunately, however, things are not so simple, and Taylor's claim loses all credibility under any sort of critical examination. For a start, one of the most characteristic human activities is precisely to reflect on the deeper meaning of our lives and to ask what it all means, if anything. It is not just philosophers who ask these sorts of questions. The question of whether there is a larger meaning to the various activities we pursue cannot be evaded simply by claiming that the meaning of our lives is within us.

To make matters even worse for Taylor's rosy optimism, it is a sad fact that many (probably most) people do not find lasting happiness or satisfaction in the tasks and accomplishments of this life. Indeed, this has often been most apparent in the lives of those who have succeeded most spectacularly in terms of cultural achievement. Recall Russell's words above when he confessed to "searching for something beyond what the world contains, something transfigured and infinite," despite his belief that it was not to be found. Russell certainly speaks for many people in his admission in the quote above that he could not help but want more than this life offers.

These observations alone completely undermine Taylor's claim that his account of the meaning of life "far exceeds in both its beauty and its permanence any heaven of which men have ever dreamed or yearned for." I dare say that the vision of heaven in Revelation and the dreams of perfect happiness it has inspired far surpass Taylor's picture, to put it mildly.

But one other glaring problem must be emphasized. Even if the activities of this life were perfectly satisfying and we performed them with as much blissful contentment as Sisyphus in the scenario where the gods have inserted a substance in his veins, the harsh fact remains that on the atheistic view of reality, things are still coming to a tragic end. Every generation dies off, and at some time in the future the human race will make its final trip up the hill and push its final stone to the top. The last civilization will be destroyed, and the hill itself will be leveled.

In view of this bleak outlook, it is altogether mystifying how Taylor can say with a straight face that his view of meaning exceeds in permanence any heaven of which men have ever dreamed. Indeed, his comment sounds more like an ironic joke than a serious statement, although he did not intend it that way. The reality is that his version of human meaning is, at the end of the day, utterly fragile and poignantly impermanent and transient. Individuals enjoy a meaningful life for several decades at best, and the human race as a whole with all its various projects will at some point come to a screeching halt. There is nothing permanent about that scenario except its utter finality for conscious life, which no one will even be around to witness.

Our Lives Are Absurd *Because* We Are Great

This brings us to another interesting maneuver to make the best of a bad situation. Contemporary philosopher Thomas Nagel has suggested that we have no reason either to be distressed about the transience of life or to be defiant or angry about it. He recommends as a better alternative that we recognize and embrace the irony of our lot.

This is what he means. The only reason our lives may seem absurd or meaningless is precisely because we have the ability to step back, as it were, and examine our lives from the outside. Here is how he puts it: "Reference to our small size and short life span and to the fact that all of mankind will eventually vanish without a trace are metaphors for the backward step which permits us to regard ourselves from without and to find the particular form of our lives curious and slightly surprising."[10]

So why is it that we have the ability to "step back" and reflect on our lives in this fashion? It is because of the very things that make us most distinctively human and separate us from lower animals. As Nagel points out, mice have no sense of absurdity or worries that their lives may be meaningless. Nor presumably do dogs, cheetahs, or sharks.

In other words, it is only because we have more developed capacities to think, feel, imagine, and so on that we can reflect on our lives as we do and understand our mortality. With big brains and deep emotions comes the ability to imagine perfect happiness and to dream of it and long for it ("I Can Only Imagine"). Big brains also allow us to understand our universe, to understand physics and cosmology. And unfortunately this leads us to the sad fact that death and destruction is the inevitable fate that awaits all of us. If we were less intelligent and did not feel deep emotions, we would not even be aware of this, let alone be disturbed by it. But since we enjoy advanced intelligence, the irony of the situation is that we can dream of and aspire to a kind of happiness that outstrips reality. We can conceive of it and dream of it, but it is only the product of our rich imagination.

In short, then, one of the inevitable "side effects" of intellectual and emotional sophistication is a sense of the absurdity of our lives. But since our intellectual and emotional sophistication is the very thing that makes us human and gives our lives richness and depth, we should not be unduly bothered by the sense of absurdity that comes with it. Rather, we should embrace the irony and live with it. "If a sense of the absurd is a way of perceiving our true situation (even though the situation is not absurd until the perception arises), then what reason can we have to resent or escape it."[11]

Nagel's move here is an ingenious one, and he is to be congratulated for his clever attempt to convert a humbling weakness into a strength. Still, I want to underscore the price to be paid for "perceiving our true situation" as Nagel sees it. What we are faced with is a brutal choice between truth and beauty, between reality and our dreams. Nagel's version of embracing the ironic truth comes at the cost of signing the death warrant for our aspirations for ultimate meaning and happiness. Highlighting the irony of this painful choice does little to make it more palatable.

"Get a Life!"

This brings us to yet another attempt to salvage the meaning of life without heaven. This is from Keith Parsons, a contemporary philosopher who has responded rather forcefully to the argument that our lives are ultimately meaningless if they are only an infinitesimal moment compared to the history of the cosmos as a whole, which stretches over billions of years. Parsons thinks it is not only arrogant but also question begging to think that our lives must be everlasting in order to be fully meaningful. Christians simply assume that a life cannot be fully meaningful unless it is everlasting, and, as he sees it, this is highly presumptuous.

Parsons vigorously rejects this assumption and thinks the lesson to be drawn from the brevity of our lives is a very different one.

> Why not draw the reverse conclusion and say that, since we know life is fleeting, we should strive to experience all the meaning we can in that short compass? The message we should draw from our mortality is this: You have a limited number of days, hours, and minutes. Therefore, you should strive to fill each of those days, hours, and minutes with meaning. You should strive to fill them with learning and gaining wisdom—with compassion for the less fortunate, with love for friends and family, with doing a job well, with fighting against evil and obscurantism, and yes, with enjoying sex, TV, pizza, and ballgames.[12]

Now what I find particularly interesting here is the suggestion that the fleeting nature of our lives can actually charge our lives with meaning rather than detract from it or even destroy it altogether. I am not sure if Parsons means to go this far with his claim, but I have heard atheists claim that our lives are *more* meaningful precisely because our time is short. So what about this claim that finitude actually has a positive impact on meaning rather than a negative one?

Before answering this I want to make clear that I would not presume to say that Parsons's life is meaningless since he does not believe in heaven. Moreover, I heartily celebrate everything he cites that brings meaning to his life. Anyone who follows his advice and seeks to fill his or her days with the sorts of things he mentions will likely experience a lot of fun, pleasure, and deep satisfaction. (The fact that his call for fighting evil is bound to be a losing cause in the long run is no doubt a bit of a downer, but I'll let that pass for the moment.) I will also grant that knowing we have only so many years, days, and hours gives us a reason to treasure every moment and make the most of every single one of them.

But having conceded this, I want to go on to argue that even a life that is as rich in meaning as Parsons describes could not be as fully meaningful and satisfying as one that comes to a heavenly end. Consider again the harsh reality that everything Parsons cherishes and enjoys is destined to come to an end, both in his personal life and in the universe as a whole. Can anyone who holds his view honestly say that the inevitable prospect of death and oblivion does not cast a dark shadow over life and detract from our joy?

Parsons seems to think not. Indeed, he alleges that anyone who thinks our lives should survive the death that will overcome the rest of the cosmos has an inflated sense of self-importance: "Surely there is something monstrously egocentric in thinking that my life is of such transcendent significance that I should be an exception to cosmic law—that my ego should survive when planets, stars, and galaxies are no more. As for anyone who really worries about the ultimate 'death' of the universe, the best advice would be 'Get a life!'"[13] At one level I resonate with Parsons when he stresses that we should value and properly appreciate this life, bounded as it is by birth and by death. However, I still see serious problems with his claims here.

First, I do not agree that the aspiration to survive death is egocentric. Recall Nagel's point discussed just above that our sense of absurdity owing to our short life span is precisely the product of what makes us distinctively human, namely, our mental and emotional capacities. It is our powers of perception and self-awareness, powers that the planets, stars, and galaxies do not have, that generate our longing to survive death. We know we are dying, but the stars and planets do not. We feel the poignancy of this, but they do not. That does not make us egotistic, as Pascal pointed out centuries ago.

> Man is only a reed, the weakest in nature, but he is a thinking reed. There is no need for the whole universe to take up arms to crush him: a vapour, a drop of water is enough to kill him. But even if the universe were to crush him, man would still be nobler than his slayer, because he knows that he is dying and the advantage the universe has over him. The universe knows none of this.[14]

Moreover, from a properly formed biblical perspective, the Christian hope is not to survive as Lone Rangers while the rest of the universe suffers death. Rather, as noted in the previous chapter, the Christian hope is for the redemption of the entire created order. We look forward to the day when this earth and all the fallen stars will be resurrected to life. So again, the Christian hope is not egotistic in the sense that Parsons claims it is.

But there is another glaring issue here. Does it really make rational or emotional sense to cherish the things Parsons mentions while being indifferent to their long-term survival? His advice to us if we worry about the death of the universe is to "Get a life!" Well, suppose someone takes his advice, gets a life, and as a result comes to love and relish all the things that give his life meaning. Is it not the case that the more a person "has a life," the more he will be concerned about the prospect of the whole thing coming to utter ruin?

Think about the sorts of things that make Parsons's life meaningful. Can he honestly say he loves these things and takes delight in them but has no sense of deep regret at the thought of losing them forever in the not-so-distant future? Suppose someone said, "I dearly love my family and friends, and I enjoy my job and take great satisfaction in doing it well; and I love a good football game (any game Notre Dame wins) on a late fall afternoon; and I love my roadster; and a great grilled salmon; and a perfectly brewed cup of Assam tea on a cold morning; and of course sex, everyone loves great sex." Well, nothing surprising there. Most people could make a similar speech.

But suppose he then went on to say the following: "As much as I love all these things, I am totally cool with the fact that it's all going to come crashing down at some point. And when it does, I realize I will not get to see how my granddaughter's life turns out, will never read or write another book, never again see the Irish beat USC, never again hear 'Gimme Shelter' as I drive my roadster on backcountry roads at dusk, never again savor salmon or a perfect cup of tea, and never again look into the eyes of the woman I love. But seriously, I'm fine with that." Would that make sense to you? Or would you think there was a huge disconnect between these two statements? The answer to me seems obvious.

In saying this, I do not mean to deny that one could end his life with a deep sense of gratitude for such wonderful things, even if he believed he would never experience them again. But unless one simply became bored with life or cynical, or these pleasures lost their zest, the point remains that the more one enjoys and finds meaning in them, the more pain he must feel in the face of their final loss and ruin. Indeed, the more one "has a life" and takes satisfaction in it, the more he must prefer that it continue and feel the tragedy of losing it forever.

I'm Satisfied without Heaven . . . but I Wish It Were True . . .

All of this reminds me of some thoughts I read several years ago from Carl Sagan, the famous agnostic astronomer. He died at age sixty-two of a rare disease, but six times prior to this he had been threatened by death. Over these years, he had often been asked how he could face his own death without the hope of an afterlife. In response, he claimed it was not a problem for him. He quoted with approval a passage from Einstein in which the famous physicist said he could not believe in any sort of God who would punish or reward us after death, or who even had a will anything like ours. Einstein claimed he had no desire to survive his physical death and continued as follows: "I am satisfied with the mystery of the eternity of life and a glimpse of the marvelous structure of the existing world, together with the devoted striving to comprehend a portion, be it ever so tiny, of the Reason that manifests itself in nature."[15] Sagan endorsed these lines as his answer to why he could face death without the hope of any sort of afterlife.

But here is what I find both intriguing and telling. As his death actually drew near, he shared some other thoughts that were quite different. He reported that his previous brushes with death had not in any way weakened his will to live. To the contrary, he continued to love life, and as he stared his imminent death in the face, he wrote movingly of aspirations he would never see fulfilled. He dearly loved his wife and would have liked to grow old with her. He would have liked to see his younger children grow up, to nurture them, and to help shape their education. He would have liked to see grandchildren yet to be conceived. He was fascinated by scientific and technological advances and would have liked to see what discoveries yet lay in the future. He was interested in political issues and would have liked to see how history would continue to unfold and how various conflicts would be resolved. The realization that he would miss out on all this was a painful thought indeed.

As he reflected on this, Sagan admitted, "I would love to believe that when I die, I will live again, that some thinking, feeling, remembering part of me will continue." A page later, Sagan went on to add, "If there were life after death, I might, no matter when I die, satisfy most of these deep curiosities and longings. But if death is nothing more than an endless sleep, this is a forlorn hope."[16]

Here is what I find telling. On the one hand, Sagan claimed to be satisfied with what this life offers, with getting just a glimpse of the structure of this world and striving to understand even a tiny portion of the natural world. But on the other hand, he admitted to yearning for more, to wishing he could in fact believe in life after death and enjoy whatever further adventures that life might offer.

Of course, he claimed he couldn't believe it, but my point is that he gave us a profoundly inconsistent account of his own desires. Since he did not believe in life after death, he professed not to wish for it and to be fully satisfied with this life. But then he admitted that he would love to believe in life after death because there was so much more he wanted to experience. A mere glimpse, it seems, was not enough for him. There is so much more beauty to see, so much more truth to learn, and so many more relationships to experience, nurture, and cherish.

Tell a Tale

The various moves we have encountered in this chapter to come to terms with the loss of heaven are all telling. Whether in the form of shriveled substitutes for heaven, claims that life is really more meaningful without it, or even the ironic observation that our frustrated yearning for ultimate meaning is a product of our advanced capacities that make us distinctively human, coming to terms with the loss of heaven is a painful operation. It requires us to stifle, even to put to death, our highest aspirations for happiness and meaning and convince ourselves that this world, this life, is enough.

None of these moves are sufficient to provide a truly comic ending to the human story. Indeed, the specter of tragedy looms large despite all these various attempts to salvage meaning for our lives. For according to all of them, our aspiration for ultimate meaning is futile, and all that we love must be destroyed if the physical universe and the laws of nature are ultimate reality.

The Nobel Prize–winning physicist Steven Weinberg has embraced tragedy itself as a sort of buffer against the threat of absurdity. In his view, greater understanding of physical reality provides at best a small measure of meaning to our lives. He writes, "The more the universe seems comprehensible, the more it also seems pointless. . . . The effort to understand the universe is one of the very few things that lifts human life a little above the level of a farce, and gives it some of the grace of a tragedy."[17]

A farce, of course, is a joke, an absurdly improbable story. Weinberg does not think human life is a farce, but it is only a little better as he sees it. This is small consolation indeed. There is, to be sure, a certain grace in tragedy, a poignant sort of beauty. But as a substitute for the grace of comedy, it falls immeasurably short—indeed, absurdly so.

3

IF GOD IS LOVE,
WHY IS THERE A HELL?

There are only two kinds of people in the end: those who say to God, "Thy will be done," and those to whom God says, in the end, "*Thy* will be done." All that are in Hell, choose it. Without that self-choice there could be no Hell. No soul that seriously and constantly desires joy will ever miss it.

—C. S. Lewis[1]

I have been arguing that the Christian drama is not only a great comedy but also a great love story. It is because the ultimate nature of reality is Love that Christians anticipate a comic end to the story. If ultimate reality is matter and the laws of physics, however, the story seems destined to come to a bad end.

"But," the critic may ask, "what about hell? How can a comedy include hell?" This is a question that cannot be ignored. At this point we have to face the fact that the Christian drama seems to include an element of the tragic that cannot be swept under the rug.

Indeed, hell is interjected by way of vivid contrast, right in the middle of that great vision of heaven in Revelation 21. Just after reading the promise of water from the spring of life for those who are thirsty and the promise that those who overcome will inherit the joys of heaven, including the ultimate joy of knowing God, we come to these sober words: "But the cowardly, the unbelieving, the vile, the murderers, the sexually immoral, those who practice magic arts, the idolaters and all liars—their place will be in the fiery lake of burning sulfur. This is the second death" (Rev. 21:8).

The fiery lake of burning sulfur and the second death seem to put a damper on the party, to put it mildly. How can hell exist if God is truly love and will bring his world to the perfect comic end we explored in the first chapter? Well, what I want to argue is that hell can exist precisely *because* God is love. Because God is love, the comic ending is assured, but because he is love, hell is also possible.

The Basic Logic of the Matter

Before exploring this more fully, let us examine the basic logic involved in the claim that hell is simply incompatible with a God of love. We can spell out the basic line of thought as follows.

1. God is perfectly good and loving as well as all-powerful.
2. If God is perfectly good and loving, he wants all persons to be saved.
3. If God is all-powerful, he can save all persons.
4. Therefore, all will be saved.

This sort of argument has often been advanced by those who hold the doctrine of universal salvation, which denies that anyone will be in hell forever. Some may go there temporarily according to some proponents of this view, but eventually all will be saved if God is perfectly loving and good as well as all-powerful.

Now the first thing to notice about this argument is that it mirrors exactly in its logic a more famous argument that evil itself is incompatible with the existence of God. We can spell this argument out as follows.

1. God is perfectly loving and good as well as all-powerful.
2. If God is perfectly loving and good, he wants there to be no evil.
3. If God is all-powerful, he can bring it about that there is no evil.
4. Therefore, there is no evil.

Obviously, evil exists. Therefore, the skeptic argues, there is no God, at least not a God who is perfectly loving and good as well as all-powerful. The existence of such a God is simply logically incompatible with the existence of evil. This, in essence, is the notorious logical problem of evil.

While this basic argument has been wielded against believers in God for centuries, one form of reply has been central to the Christian response. In particular, Christians have appealed to human free will to account for how evil can be compatible with God's existence. That is, Christian thinkers have pointed out that if God makes us truly free and gives us a significant range of free choice, then we may use our freedom to choose evil rather than good. While God prefers that we choose good, we may choose evil instead, and if we are truly free, he cannot simultaneously leave us free and prevent that evil.

I want to emphasize that the appeal to freedom does not exhaust the Christian response to evil, but it is fair to say that most philosophers and theologians believe freedom is at least central to whatever reasons God has for permitting evil. Freedom is arguably an intrinsic good, but the crucial point is that it is a necessary means to other important goods that cannot be achieved without it. So in order to achieve those goods, evil may be the price that must be paid.

The relevance of this to the problem of hell is probably already apparent. Recall that the logical argument of evil mirrors the argument that hell is incompatible with a God of love. So here is the basic point. If freedom can account for the evil *in this world*, the same freedom may explain why hell exists *in the next*. If people may use their freedom now to resist God and choose evil, they may continue to do so in the next world, and that may explain why some people are in hell forever. God may not be able to save some people, even though he is willing to do so and is all-powerful. Some people may use their freedom to resist God forever.

It is important to be clear that on this account of hell, no one is there against his or her wishes. Rather, people are there entirely because of their own choices. C. S. Lewis has famously summed up this view of hell in the following words: "I willingly believe that the damned are, in one sense, successful, rebels to the end; that the doors of hell are locked on the *inside*."[2] This, of course, is very much at odds with many popular views of hell that picture the lock on the *outside*. That is to say, those in hell want to come out, but God will not let them. On Lewis's view, they will not come out by their own choice.

Hell and the Great Love Story

Let us examine more carefully why hell is possible precisely because God is love. Recall from chapter 1 that original, primordial reality is love in the form of an eternal loving relationship between the Father, Son, and Holy Spirit. Jesus referred to this in his high priestly prayer when he spoke of the love his Father had for him before the world was ever created (John 17:24).

Next, reflect on these words of Jesus in light of his words from the high priestly prayer: "As the Father has loved me, so have I loved you" (John 15:9). This is an extraordinary claim in its own right, but it is all the more momentous when we recall Jesus's comment about the love the Father had for him before all creation. Jesus is saying that his love for us is an expression of that eternal trinitarian love that has existed from all eternity. The eternal dance of love and joy that is the primordial reality is lived out for us in the life, death, and resurrection of Jesus. As we see how deeply he loved, how he wept at the tomb of Lazarus, and how graciously he gave his life so that we could live, we see a fleshly portrait of the ultimate springs of truth and reality.

Consider now a third text in light of those two: "A new command I give you: Love one another. As I have loved you, so you must love one another" (John 13:34). Notice the staggering implications of this. The Father and the Son have loved each other from all eternity, before the world was ever created. Jesus, the eternal Son of God incarnate, loved us with that same kind of love. Now he commands his disciples to continue to transmit that same kind of love to each other! In other words, we are called to live out eternal trinitarian love in our relationships with each other! The eternal dance of love and joy in the Trinity should be on display in how Christians treat each other.

But here is the point I am driving at. When we come to this third text, it involves a commandment, not a simple statement of fact. It is an imperative, and as such it requires our cooperation. The first two texts pertain to the love of God, first as that love has existed from all eternity and then as that same love was shown to us by Jesus. But in this third text, we are invited, indeed commanded, to reproduce that same kind of love. But for that to happen, we must be willing to love as he loved us.

This is both exhilarating and intimidating. How, after all, can fallen, frail people like us be expected to reproduce trinitarian love in our relationships? Isn't that a fantastic notion, to put it mildly?

Well, I suppose it would be if Jesus had not commanded it. But as John Wesley observed, such divine commands are equivalent to promises.[3] So when God commands us to do something, implicit in the command is his promise that he will enable us to do it. Of course we could never love like that on our own power. But as Jesus explained, he is the vine and we are the branches. "No branch can bear fruit by itself; it must remain in the vine. Neither can you bear fruit unless you remain in me" (John 15:4).

Consider one more text from John that is relevant to this point: "If anyone loves me, he will obey my teaching. My Father will love him, and we will come to him and make our home with him. He who does not love me will not obey my teaching" (John 14:23–24a). Again, what I want to emphasize here is our free choice in this matter. Notice the conditional statement: if we love Jesus and obey his teaching, he and the Father will make their home with us!

Recall from chapter 1 that the crowning feature of heaven is that God will live with us in intimate fellowship. "Now the dwelling of God is with men, and he will live with them" (Rev. 21:3). The text from John teaches us that we can experience this in a preliminary fashion even in this life. But notice: for God to live with us, we must love and obey him. Love and obedience are closely connected, but obedience is not simply a matter of rote performance. The obedience God wants from us is an obedience that flows out of genuine love.

And this is what brings into focus the staggering reality that hell is possible precisely because God is love. For what this text also brings to light is that some may choose not to love Jesus or obey his teaching. As astounding as this is to contemplate, some human beings may refuse the gift of perfect love. They may choose not to welcome God into their lives. They may choose to reject the trinitarian God of eternal love, the Creator of the universe who gave his Son in order to give us eternal life with him.

This is what makes the connection with hell obvious. Any who choose not to love God and invite him into their lives have chosen to exclude themselves from heaven by that very choice. Remember, heaven is the ultimate experience of "God with us."

To see the force of this more clearly, let us reflect on why it is that genuine love for finite beings requires freedom. God is love by his very nature as a being who exists from all eternity in a loving relationship of three persons. He is necessarily good; indeed, he is goodness itself and cannot be tempted by evil (James 1:13). By contrast, creatures like ourselves who are made in God's image but who are still finite must freely choose to love God if our love is to be real.[4] While acts of obedience can be forced, we may still rebel. As the defiant child famously said to his father who demanded that he sit down, "I may be sitting down on the outside, but I am still standing up on the inside." So obedience is one thing; willing obedience is quite another.

Even more so, love cannot be forced. God loves us and desires our love in return. True love can be invited, elicited, and won, but it cannot be coerced, programmed, or simply demanded. When Christ commands us to love one another as he has loved us, he can do so because his love has elicited our love in return. But those who do not love him will not obey him.

It is because love is at the very heart of our freedom as creatures made in the image of God that some people may choose not to return the love of God. Rob Bell was exactly right when he wrote the following: "Love demands freedom. It always has, and it always will. We are free to resist, reject, and rebel against God's ways for us. We can have all the hell we want."[5]

And that is why it is the case, ironic though it is, that hell is possible precisely because God is love.

A Challenge: Freedom Cannot Stop God from Saving Everyone

The argument from human freedom is the one most philosophers today employ to defend the doctrine of eternal hell. However, the argument is not without its detractors, and some of its most vocal critics are other Christian thinkers who espouse the doctrine of universal salvation. I will look at two of those critics.

The first of these is Marilyn Adams, a leading Christian philosopher who was also the first female canon of Christ Church Oxford. Adams has been challenging the doctrine of eternal hell for years, and more recently she has rejected the argument from freedom for a very straightforward reason. In her view, freedom is overrated. As she sees it, it is simply misguided to think freedom is something almost sacred and so important that not even God can override it. To give human freedom this much significance is to put God and humans on the same level, almost as if they were moral peers. Adams sees this tendency particularly in those who defend hell as the natural consequence of rejecting God and the love he offers, as I have done. In her view, it is not a compliment to us to think God gives us the freedom to damn ourselves. That is not the sort of respect God should pay to mere creatures like us.

Indeed, the appeal to human freedom to defend hell points out a deeper problem according to Adams. That problem, she thinks, is that it underestimates just how enormous the "size gap" is between God and human beings. Those who appeal to free will to defend eternal hell picture the relationship between God and human beings as something like the relationship between parents and adult children. That is, we are like adult children and God is like our parent. Given this picture, it makes sense that God could hold us accountable for our choices, even if those choices lead to damnation.

Adams thinks a more accurate model is the relationship between a mother and an infant or a toddler. This model better represents the "size gap" between God and human beings. And when we think of it this way, it makes little sense to think God would not interfere with our freedom or even override it if necessary to save us from eternal hell.

Suppose a mother saw her infant child walking toward a fire. Would she leave the child alone to fall in the fire out of respect for the child's freedom? Of course not! She would intervene and prevent the child from such a serious injury.

Adams provides a more colorful example when she remarks that if God needs to overrule our freedom to save us from hell, this is "no more an insult to our dignity than a mother's changing a diaper is to a baby."[6] So on this view, sinful humans are more like babies who soil their pants than like disrespectful adult children or even rebellious teenagers. We may not want our pants changed and may kick and cry. But just as a loving mother will change the diaper with or without the baby's cooperation, God will change us, if necessary, without our free cooperation. So human freedom is no problem and will not prevent God from saving all persons.

In response to this, I certainly agree that we should not underestimate the "size gap" between God and human beings. However, I do not believe Adams's model is a good one to capture the biblical account of the divine-human relationship. Indeed, from the very beginning of the Bible, God gives commands and expects obedience. He makes covenants with people and expects them to honor those covenants. He expresses anger and disappointment when his children fail, and he holds them accountable for their sin and rebellion. None of this squares with Adams's picture of the divine-human relationship. Indeed, one of the most prominent biblical images for that relationship is that of a spouse to a husband. We are God's spouse, and he expects us to be faithful and to return his love.

But there is another problem as well for Adams's view. If God is willing to overrule our freedom, as she argues, we may wonder why he does not do it now in light of all the horrendous evil that results from the abuse of freedom. The fact that God gives us so much leeway, even at the price of so much terrible evil, gives us good reason to think that he takes our freedom more seriously than Adams suggests. Indeed, it suggests that our free choices play an important role in his purposes for creation.

In short, I do not think Adams does justice to how seriously God takes human freedom, so I am not persuaded by her critique of the freedom argument for eternal hell. The freedom to reject the love of God remains a plausible explanation for why eternal hell is possible.

But Choosing Eternal Hell Just Makes No Sense

Let us turn to another critic of the freedom view of hell, Thomas Talbott, a contemporary philosopher who has vigorously and creatively defended the view that all persons will be saved in the end. Unlike Adams, who is willing to simply dispense with human freedom if it stands in the way of God's saving some people, Talbott has tried to argue that God can save all persons without overriding their freedom.

The heart of his case is that there simply is no intelligible motive for anyone to choose eternal hell. So the idea that persons might freely choose to remain in hell forever is utterly incoherent. It makes no sense at all if carefully examined.

Now this does not mean that we cannot choose evil in the short run, for obviously we can. But Talbott thinks there is a fundamental difference between choosing evil in the short run and doing so forever. We can choose evil in the short run under the illusion that it will make us happy. The prodigal son in Jesus's parable, for instance, might serve as an example of this. He enjoyed his sinful lifestyle for a while.

However, the inevitable result of choosing evil is that it will make us miserable. The illusion that sin can make us happy will eventually be shattered, as it was for the prodigal son when he found himself broke and alone, feeding the pigs. Everyone will eventually realize it is better back home with our heavenly Father and will return to him, just as the prodigal returned to the welcoming arms of his father.

To put this a little more precisely in philosophical terms, Talbott thinks that, strictly speaking, it is logically impossible that anyone will be lost forever. This is a far stronger position than that of those who merely *hope* that all will be saved, or even that of those who think it is *probably true* that all will be saved. On Talbott's view, it is *necessarily true* that all will be saved.

So why does he take such a strong view if he does not simply dispense with freedom? Well, his view hinges crucially on a couple of central claims. First, it depends on his account of what it means to choose an eternal destiny. In short, such a choice must be fully informed in such a way that the person making it never regrets his choice. That means the person must be free of all ignorance and illusion both in his initial choice as well as later. He must fully understand what he has chosen while freely sticking with the choice.

What this shows is that there is a profound difference between choosing heaven as an eternal destiny and choosing hell. It makes perfect sense that one could choose heaven and remain happy in that choice in the long run. Those who choose heaven would never regret it. By contrast, it makes no sense that anyone could choose hell without coming to regret it at some point.

Think again of the prodigal son and the fact that he regretted his choice to leave his father by the time he was reduced to feeding the pigs. While he was initially under the illusion that he would be happier away from home, that illusion was ripped away by hard reality. If he were forced to stay in the pigpen, his choice would not be truly free. A free choice is one that is clear sighted and under no illusions.

This brings us to the second claim that is crucial for Talbott's view, that the very idea of choosing eternal hell is simply incoherent. This is the claim that the New Testament pictures hell "as a forcibly imposed punishment rather than as a freely embraced condition," a punishment that leads to "unbearable suffering."[7] Now if hell is such a forcibly imposed punishment with such a severe result, then his claim is reinforced that no one could freely choose to remain there forever.

Problems for Talbott

But the claim that hell is a forcibly imposed punishment that produces unbearable misery raises an obvious problem for Talbott. How could anyone who repented under those conditions truly be free? We can only absorb so much pain, so if hell forcibly imposes ever-greater suffering, no one could resist forever.

Suppose the prodigal son's father had secretly sent a message, along with a large bribe, to the farmer who had hired his son to feed the pigs. His message instructed the farmer to beat his son every day and to make the beatings more severe each day until he admitted he had made a mistake and decided to return home.

Now if this happened, it is clear that the prodigal son would be forced to "repent" at some point or that he would simply die under the pain of ever more severe beatings. But the question is whether "repentance" that is compelled in this fashion is sincere repentance. To be sure, painful discipline can be a means that leads to repentance. But for that to be the case, the discipline must lead to a genuine change of heart. It cannot simply be a matter of knuckling under because the pain is so great that one cannot stand it.

And here is the point. Our freedom can only bear so much pressure in this regard. At some point, if the pain is simply too intense, we would be forced to either give in or die. Repentance that is compelled in this way is not true repentance.

Talbott's Clarifications

Interestingly, Talbott recognizes this point. He has himself drawn a distinction between two kinds of compulsion and defended what he calls the "right" kind. That is the sort of compulsion that comes from dramatic conversions that are rather common in the Christian tradition. Many Christians have had powerful encounters with God that they describe in terms reminiscent of Paul's famous Damascus Road experience. In such encounters, many people feel as if they simply had no choice but to submit.

By contrast, Talbott repudiates the sort of compulsion that unfortunately has sometimes been employed by religious believers, namely, the demand to convert under threat of lethal force. The demand to "convert or die" has too often been spoken by religious believers. Talbott rejects this when he writes, "A stunning revelation such as Paul reportedly received, one that provides clear vision and *compelling evidence*, thereby altering one's beliefs in a perfectly rational way, does not compel belief in the same way that threatening with a sword might."[8]

Talbott is surely right in drawing a distinction between these two forms of compulsion. Moreover, most would agree that the latter form of compulsion is not only morally objectionable but also incompatible with any meaningful freedom. Conversion at sword point is not likely to be a freely chosen decision.

In the same vein, Talbott has also clarified what he means by a "forcibly imposed punishment" that produces "unbearable suffering." To illustrate what he means, he offers us the example of a foolish married man who has an affair with an unstable woman and then ends the relationship. Later, as an act of revenge for ending the relationship, the woman murders his wife and child. Talbott says the man's subsequent guilt, sorrow, and profound sense of loss would constitute unbearable suffering for him. God could use this suffering for good, and "insofar as God uses the man's suffering as a means of correction, or as means of encouraging repentance, we can say that the man has endured a *forcibly imposed punishment* for his sin."[9]

But the Problems Remain: Is His Repentance Inevitable?

So what about this example of the foolish philanderer? We can readily grant that his actions and the subsequent course of events cause him great misery. But the question remains whether it is *inevitable* that he will turn back to God. Surely God can use his suffering as a means of correction to *encourage* repentance, as Talbott notes. But still, there is nothing in the case as described that makes such a response *inevitable* or *necessary*.

Indeed, we can easily imagine that instead of repenting, the philanderer might become angry and embittered if he believes God allowed the murder of his wife and baby as a means of punishment for his affair. He might judge this a disproportionate punishment for his sin and come to see God as a vengeful deity who does not deserve worship and obedience. And as a result, he might move ever farther away from God in his rebellion, hardening his heart more by every step.

This is all the more plausible in view of Talbott's opinion that we have the freedom, "expressed in thousands of specific choices, to move incrementally either in the direction of repentance and reconciliation or in the direction of greater separation from God, and that freedom God always respects."[10] Now if this is true, it is far from clear why such incremental movement, one inch at a time, must inevitably shatter our illusions in such a way that we could not but repent and be reconciled to God.

Indeed, it seems that just the opposite would be the case. With every step we take away from God, the farther we are removed from him. These steps add up and over time can cover quite a distance. Likewise, the more we harden our heart and dull our conscience, the more we will form a character that is comfortable with sin. Again, little acts add up to form a character. And the more we have a character that is comfortable with sin, the less we will be inclined to repent and be reconciled to God.

Objectively speaking, any person who had such a character would be miserable. But *subjectively*, in the realm of feeling and experience, the hardness of heart would make the misery more tolerable. So the upshot is that Talbott's example is not a convincing case of unbearable suffering.

Two Kinds of Compulsion: A Hell of a Dilemma

But let us turn now to Talbott's distinction between two different forms of compulsion and his claim that "compelling evidence" represents the "right" kind of compulsion. That is to say, God can present us with powerful evidence that will compel us to repent, and there is nothing objectionable about that.

I am very dubious, however, that evidence is ever compelling, strictly speaking. This is especially so when we are dealing with matters as controversial as religious beliefs. The reason this is so is because belief is far more than a matter of the intellect. Our emotions, will, and desires are also involved. And if we are unwilling to repent, we cannot be compelled to do so by evidence.

This is not to deny that there is good evidence in favor of religious belief. But my point is that there is a vast difference between *adequate* evidence and *compelling* evidence. Indeed, the Bible has numerous examples of people who were presented with very impressive evidence but did not believe. The Israelites witnessed striking miracles in their deliverance from Egypt but later showed a heart of rebellion and unbelief. Likewise, in the New Testament, not everyone who witnessed miracles or had good evidence for them repented or accepted Christ.

Unfortunately for Talbott, then, neither "compelling evidence" nor "unbearable suffering" can guarantee that all persons will repent and be saved. Evidence is never, strictly speaking, compelling in the relevant sense. And any suffering that is truly "unbearable" would represent the wrong sort of compulsion. It would not bring genuine repentance. And the example of "unbearable suffering" that Talbott gives us is not literally unbearable. Rather, it might just as easily produce more rebellion and hardness of heart that would lead a person farther away from God and make him more comfortable in his sin.

Of course, God could also cause increasing pain to us in other ways as we move farther and farther away from him. He could, like a Spanish inquisitor, forcibly impose greater and greater physical pain upon us—tighten the screws, so to speak, with each such incremental move. And were he to do this, then surely we would reach a point where we would crack. But presumably Talbott would reject this as the "wrong" kind of compulsion.

So Talbott faces a dilemma, indeed, a hell of a dilemma. He must either give up his claim that the misery of hell is unbearable or he must affirm a form of compulsion he has repudiated. If the only sort of suffering God imposes on those in hell is like that of the foolish philanderer, there is no reason why sinners may not continue to rebel and resist him forever. But if God imposes ever-greater misery to the point that it is literally unbearable, then he would be using the sort of compulsion Talbott rejects. It appears, then, that sinners can freely resist God forever, contrary to Talbott's argument.

But What about the Rich Man and Lazarus?

Let's continue to explore these points in light of a famous biblical description of hell, namely, the story of the rich man and Lazarus. This story is relevant to our discussion in the first place because Talbott cites it as evidence for the view that hell is forcibly imposed punishment.[11] It is also interesting from another angle, however, since I have often heard it cited against the freedom defense of hell. What this story shows, it is alleged, is that the rich man sincerely repents, but his repentance is rejected because it is too late. So the reason that hell is eternal is not because the doors of hell are locked on the inside, as Lewis would have it. To the contrary, it is eternal because its inhabitants are forced to stay there against their wishes, even though they would gladly repent and receive salvation if they could.

Now it is worth noting that this story may be a parable. But whether it is or not, we cannot press all the details of the story and assume each of them is intended to teach a specific lesson. The point I want to emphasize, however, is that there are other viable interpretations of the story. These interpretations support neither Talbott's view of hell nor the view that the inhabitants of hell are forced to stay there despite their sincere repentance.

First, there is nothing in the story to indicate that the misery of the rich man was an unbearable punishment that led to his repentance and eventual salvation. That is precisely the scenario we would expect if Talbott's theory of hell is correct. Contrary to this, the "great gulf" that separates the rich man from Lazarus remains between them, without any indication that it will inevitably be traversed at some point.

Second, despite the rich man's misery, he seems more concerned to justify himself than to truly repent and sincerely throw himself on God's mercy. Although his first request is for relief from his pain, his next request is for Lazarus to be sent to his brothers to warn them so they can escape his fate.

Think about that for a moment. What does it imply? While this appears on the surface to be a loving gesture on behalf of his brothers, I would suggest that it may equally well be understood as an indirect attempt at self-justification. That is to say, the rich man seems to be hinting in his request that if he had been better informed and warned, *he would not be there either*. Indeed, his demand is arguably for compelling evidence, the very sort of thing that Talbott thinks would be convincing and move all sinners to repentance.

But, third, notice that that suggestion is countered by Abraham's response when he points out that his brothers have Moses and the Prophets. When the rich man retorts that more is needed, that they would repent if someone from the dead went to them, Abraham rejects this out of hand: "If they do not listen to Moses and the Prophets, they will not be convinced even if someone rises from the dead" (Luke 16:31). The point seems clear that the rich man is not in hell because he lacked sufficient evidence. Just like his brothers, he had available to him Moses and the Prophets. And Moses and the Prophets warned against indifference to the poor, yet the rich man ignored Lazarus as he lay at his gate covered with sores. In other words, he had more than enough evidence but declined to act on the truth that was clearly in front of him.

Moreover, he is continuing to justify himself rather than truly repent. As I see it, then, hell is indeed a place of misery but not unbearable misery. This is why it can be freely chosen forever as one's eternal destiny.

The Misery Paradox: So Close and Yet So Far Away

Let us reflect further on the nature of this misery by pondering a puzzle that was raised to me about two seemingly inconsistent descriptions of hell. The question was posed to me as follows: "Revelation 14:9–11 portrays the eternal torment of the condemned as taking place 'in the presence of the holy angels and in the presence of the Lamb' (14:10). What does this mean? And how should we understand the portrayal in relation to other traditional images of hell as banishment from the presence of Christ?"[12] So the question is how the suffering of hell can take place in the presence of Christ if the essence of hell is being separated from God. Isn't this contradictory?

Well, in response to this, I'd start with the observation of the psalmist that there is no place where we can successfully flee from God's presence (Ps. 139:7–11). The God of love is everywhere, and we cannot exist a millisecond without his sustaining grace and power. Paul makes a similar point in his sermon at Mars Hill, where he reminds his listeners that God is "not far from each one of us. 'For in him we live, and move and have our being'" (Acts 17:27–28).

This latter text is particularly relevant, for Paul is applying this point to people who may be seeking God but have not yet found him. The point here, then, is that even people who may be "far" from God in terms of a meaningful, loving relationship are still "close" to him in the sense that he continually sustains them in existence.

So the unhappy creatures described in Revelation 14 are in the presence of the Lamb by virtue of the fact that he sustains them in existence, and they may even be aware of this fact. However, they are utterly separated from him by their sinful rebellion. They are close in terms of something like proximity, but far apart in terms of mutual love and intimacy.

It is easy to see how this uneasy situation causes misery. Imagine a son alienated from his father who deeply loves him. He hates his father and resents the fact that he is dependent upon him, so he will not return his love but is forced by unhappy circumstances to live under the same roof with him. The misery in this case would be palpable.

Indeed, the paradoxical nature of this observation may illumine why fire is used as an image of the torments of hell. Fire in the Bible is a common image for the presence of God, not his absence (cf. Deut. 4:24; 5:24–25; Ps. 50:3; Heb. 12:29). But his presence is experienced very differently by those who are rightly related to him, as opposed to those who are not.

David Bentley Hart has noted that there is a long theological tradition, particularly in Eastern Orthodoxy, that "makes no distinction, essentially, between the fire of hell and the light of God's glory, and that interprets damnation as the soul's resistance to the beauty of God's glory, its refusal to open itself before the divine love, which causes divine love to seem an exterior chastisement."[13]

Perhaps we can take this a step further and suggest that this may explain why the frightful passage about the lake of fire (Rev. 21:8) appears right in the middle of the most glorious description of the Holy City in the whole Bible. And indeed, this is right after the beautiful picture of the spring of the water of life given to those who are thirsty (Rev. 21:6). As Robert Mulholland has pointed out, "if, as John says, those in hell are in fire in the presence of the Lamb (14:10), who in the vision is seated on the throne with God (7:17), and the Water of Life flows from the throne (22:1), then both the fire image and the water image are linked to the throne."[14]

Again, our freedom allows us to refuse his love and go our own way, even as it remains true that "in him we live and move and have our being." if that is our choice, his glorious love will be experienced like a burning fire rather than "the spring of the water of life" that will deeply quench our thirst.

But Seriously, Why Would Anyone Choose Eternal Hell?

Still, there is something deeply perplexing if not unintelligible about such a choice, and Talbott certainly raises an obvious question in asking what possible motive could explain it. What can we say to this?

I readily grant that the idea of any rational person choosing eternal hell is hard to conceive of. Indeed, there is something deeply irrational in such a choice, and we cannot fully make sense of it. I wrote my PhD dissertation on hell several years ago, and this was one of the most difficult challenges I faced in defending the doctrine. It still leaves me baffled to this day. Nevertheless,

I believe the choice of hell does have its own sort of logic, and we can make at least *some* sense of it, although not entirely.

For a start, I would encourage anyone who wrestles with this question to read C. S. Lewis's little book *The Great Divorce*. For those who have never read it, the premise of the book is that a group of "ghosts" from hell take a bus ride to heaven and are invited—indeed, implored—to stay. Common sense says they would jump at the offer. But contrary to common sense, almost all the ghosts reject the invitation and return to hell.

What is most striking about the book is how Lewis describes these characters in such a way that makes psychological and emotional sense of their choice to return to hell. I often urge people to read that book in conjunction with another of Lewis's books, *The Four Loves*. One of the main points of that book is that the love between human beings will go bad and even become demonic if it is not transformed by divine love. Human love is not sufficient to sustain itself and remain strong without being properly related to God, the ultimate source of all love.

One of the most poignant examples of this occurs near the end of *The Great Divorce*. There we meet a character from hell who arrives in heaven to meet his wife, who is named Sarah Smith. She was a very loving person even during this life, although she acknowledges that much of her love for her husband had been motivated by her own need to be loved. Such "need love," as Lewis calls it, is a genuine form of love, but it is easy to see how it can become twisted and abused. Healthy need can easily become "needy," and this can be exploited and abused by selfish persons.

Although her love had not always been perfect, as she confesses, she had allowed her human love to be fully transformed by God's perfect love. She is now radiant with love and joy and is no longer vulnerable to unhealthy manipulation.

By contrast, her husband was a person who used human love to manipulate others and to get his way. Thereby, his love was actually deformed into a perverse kind of hatred. Even as a child, he would pout and sulk when he did not get his way. He knew his sisters would feel bad for him and eventually give in, because they could not stand for him to have his feelings hurt.

He continued this pattern in marriage, and indeed, as he talks with his wife, it is apparent that he is still bent on using love as a weapon to cause her pain. In particular, he assumes that his wife must be miserable without him, since he has been in hell all that time. She explains to him, however, that in heaven, all needs are satisfied and all love is pure. So while she loves him, he can no longer use that love to manipulate her or hurt her. He cannot destroy her happiness by sulking in hell. She urges him to embrace true love and to remain in heaven, where he can be truly happy.

As she makes this appeal, he feels the force of it at least to some degree, and it appears that he will repent of his sins and choose to remain in heaven. Lewis describes this as follows.

> Her beauty brightened so that I could hardly see anything else, and under that sweet compulsion the Dwarf [her husband] really looked at her for the first time. . . . And really, for a moment, I thought the Dwarf was going to obey: partly because the outlines of his face became a little clearer, and partly because the invitation to all joy, singing out of her whole being like a bird's song on an April evening, seemed to me such that no creature could resist it.[15]

Now I find particularly interesting here Lewis's use of the phrase "sweet compulsion" in light of our earlier discussion of the two different kinds of compulsion. This "sweet compulsion" is not a matter of using threats or lethal force. Sarah Smith's "weapons" are love, joy, and beauty, and she aims straight for the heart.

And yet as hard as it may seem to resist such compulsion, resist he does, although at times he nearly gives in. The narrator doubts that he "ever saw anything more terrible than the struggle of that Dwarf Ghost against joy."[16] However, what he refuses to give up is the perverse pleasure he takes in the sense that he is in control and she still needs him. As she attempts to reason with him, urging him to stay, he continues to cling to the illusion that she is doing it because it will hurt her if he does not stay. "'Ah, you cannot bear it!' he shouted with miserable triumph."[17]

The phrase "miserable triumph" perhaps encapsulates as well as anything the perverse logic that makes some sort of sense of how eternal hell can be freely chosen. No one who chooses to remain in bitterness, resentment, and alienation from those who love him or her is truly happy. And yet bitterness and resentment do offer a certain form of pleasure, twisted though it is. Those who cling to such pleasure may do so with a sense of triumph, illusory as it is, even as they defiantly lock the doors of hell from the inside, thereby remaining "in one sense, successful, rebels to the end."

The Rich Man and the Dwarf

I would suggest that the rich man in Jesus's story and the dwarf in *The Great Divorce* have something in common. They remain in hell because neither one has embraced true repentance, and neither one has a heart that is open to the transforming love of God. As a result, they experience the love and glory of God as a painful fire, and the joy of other persons only causes them grief. Both cling to a sense of being aggrieved and attempt to manipulate feelings of pity. And both take a sense of satisfaction in those feelings, perverse as they are.

Generally speaking, the reason hell can be freely chosen is that it is a distorted mirror image of heaven. There is no righteousness or holiness in hell, but it does offer the alternative of self-righteousness. It offers no real joy or happiness, but it does offer the deformed sense of satisfaction from holding on to bitterness, resentment, and hurt. There is no real fulfillment, but it does offer the illusory triumph of getting one's way, self-destructive though it is.

Hell is the empty shell of which heaven is the pulsating, vibrant reality. But the shell is not without its pleasures, miserable though they are.

IF WE ARE SAVED BY GRACE,
WHY DO WE NEED PURGATORY?

> The whole operation of Purgatory is directed to the freeing
> of the judgment and the will. . . . Purgatory is the resolute
> breaking down, at whatever cost, of the prison walls, so
> that the soul may be able to emerge at last into liberty and
> endure unscathed the unveiled light of reality.
>
> Dorothy L. Sayers[1]

There is no point in ignoring the elephant in the room, something I am seldom disposed to do anyway. And there is no ducking the fact that *purgatory* is a fighting word. Indeed, the doctrine has generated intense reaction from Protestants for centuries. Consider, for instance, Calvin's take on purgatory. In his view, purgatory is a lie of the devil, an attempt to find salvation from our sins somewhere else instead of the blood of Christ.

Therefore, we must cry out with the shout not only of our voices but of our throats and lungs that purgatory is a deadly fiction of Satan, which nullifies the cross of Christ, inflicts unbearable contempt upon God's mercy, and overturns and destroys our faith. For what means this purgatory of theirs but that satisfaction for sins is paid by the souls of the dead after their death?[2]

As Calvin saw it, purgatory must be loudly rejected by all persons who trust the blood of Christ for their salvation.

Of course, we must remember Calvin's historical context—namely, that he lived and carried out his ministry during that crucial but volatile period of church history known as the Protestant Reformation. The doctrine of purgatory was at the heart of the controversies that split the Western church. This is largely because purgatory was a powerful fund-raising tool at the time, and the abuses surrounding it were rampant. In particular, the Roman Church was selling "indulgences," which promised that those who purchased them could free themselves or their loved ones from the punishment of purgatory. The most notorious purveyor of indulgences was a monk by the name of Tetzel, who is famous for this couplet:

> As soon as the coin in the coffer rings,
> The soul from purgatory springs.[3]

These lines are surely among the most infamous in all of history, and they symbolize the historic Protestant disdain for the doctrine of purgatory.

Given that purgatory was so intimately connected with the abuse and corruption of the Roman Church at the time, it is hardly surprising that Christians who endorse the Reformation instinctively respond negatively to the doctrine. Indeed, the long shadows of Tetzel are still with us, and, understandably, they continue to cast the doctrine in a dubious light for many Protestants.

But the real Protestant objections to purgatory go much deeper than the abuse of the doctrine for financial gain or other dubious causes. No one should be under the illusion that these can be ignored or easily overcome. However, some Protestant thinkers have recently shown a willingness to reconsider the doctrine, and a few have endorsed carefully qualified versions of it. I myself, of course, have argued at length for an ecumenical version of the doctrine that is compatible with Protestant theology. More recently, from the Roman Catholic side, Brett Salkeld has published a book entitled *Can Catholics and Evangelicals Agree about Purgatory and the Last Judgment?* In that book, he argues that there is reason to hope the answer is yes. There are, then, some positive signs that the time may be ripe for an ecumenical version of the doctrine to gain wider acceptance.

Despite these positive signs, the general Protestant and evangelical attitude is still negative, often sharply so. Shortly after I published my book, the online journal *Credo* devoted an issue to the subject, asking whether purgatory is an evangelical doctrine.[4] My book came under considerable fire in that issue, and the resounding answer these critics gave was an unequivocal no, for the same sort of reasons given by Calvin in the quote above.

As many evangelicals see it, then, the doctrine is at odds with the Protestant doctrine of salvation by grace through faith alone. It is, moreover, an insult to the work of Christ on the cross. I shall come back to these matters, but before doing so I want to spell out why many Christian thinkers through the ages have believed we need a doctrine of purgatory. Only if we are clear about this can we properly assess the doctrine.

Every Theology Needs Purgatory

So here are the basic facts every theology needs to account for. First, heaven is a place of total perfection, full of light, beauty, and goodness. Nothing impure or unclean can enter there (Rev. 21:27). To enter heaven, we must be completely holy. The book of Hebrews urges us to "pursue peace with everyone, and the holiness without which no one will see the Lord" (Heb. 12:14 NRSV).

Notice a couple things about this holiness. In the first place, it is necessary to see the Lord. It is not optional nor merely a recommendation for "super saints" that the rest of us can ignore. Moreover, even though the persons to whom the author is writing are Christians, he does not assume they are already holy in the sense he has in mind. That is why he urges them to pursue holiness. It is essential to see the Lord, but they do not already possess it, at least not fully.

To use a classic theological term, those in heaven must be fully perfect in character in such a way that they are "impeccable," which means they can no longer sin. Doing evil must be impossible for the redeemed in heaven.

Now here is the second basic fact. The great majority of persons—all, according to many theological traditions—are far from perfect when they die. This is true despite the fact that they are justified, forgiven by God, and restored to a right relationship with him. And it is true despite the fact that they have been regenerated by the Holy Spirit and made a new creation in Christ. Indeed, this is true even on the assumption that everyone has made at least some progress in the pursuit of holiness, some more than others. The obvious fact remains that most are not completely holy, let alone impeccable, when they die.

So, in brief, here is the question. What do we say about the second of these facts in light of the first fact? Well, there are broadly three possibilities. First, we could say that anyone who is less than fully perfect when he or she dies is lost and goes to hell. Second, we could say that God will instantly perfect us at the moment of death as an act of sovereign grace. He could simply zap us and thereby perfect us. Third, we could say that God will continue the sanctification process after death with our free cooperation until we are fully and completely perfect.

We can rule out the first option rather quickly. It has been held by some Christians but is a tiny minority view, and I shall not consider it any further. The real contest is between options

2 and 3. Option 2 is the view held by most Protestants, and option 3 is held by Roman Catholics, Eastern Orthodox, and a minority of Protestants.

But either way we go on this matter, we have to have some sort of doctrine of purgatory. Consider this quote from John Fletcher, an Anglican theologian of the eighteenth century: "If we understand by *purgatory*, the manner in which souls, still polluted with the remains of sin, are, or may be *purged* from those remains, that they may see a holy God, and dwell with him forever; the question, *Which is the true purgatory?* is by no means frivolous: for it is the grand inquiry, *How shall I be eternally saved?* proposed in different expressions."[5] Fletcher's point is that every system of theology must have an account of how we are "purged" from the remains of sin.

On the view of most Protestants, this purging takes place in an instant, whereas for Roman Catholics and others, it requires an ongoing process that still requires time. But both views have a doctrine of "purgatory" in the sense that they provide an account of how the remains of sin are purged and we are made completely holy and impeccable in our character.

In the rest of this chapter, I want to argue that for Protestant theology as well as Roman Catholic, a version of the doctrine of purgatory as a continuing process after death makes better sense than the more common view that we are instantly perfected at death. Before doing so, however, we need to distinguish clearly between two very different views of the nature and purpose of purgatory. Not all accounts of purgatory are the same, as we shall see.

Satisfaction and Sanctification

As already noted, the word *purgatory* comes from the word *purge* and pertains to the idea of purging or cleansing imperfections or impurities. It can also suggest the idea of purging disease or harmful substances from one's body, so purgatory can be thought of in terms of healing what is unhealthy or ill.

So whether the image is that of cleansing or healing, purgatory is about a forward-looking process of perfecting that which is imperfect. Understood in these terms, the essential purpose of purgatory is sanctification. It is about completing the work of making us truly and fully holy. Purgatory is the successful end of the pursuit of that holiness without which no one can see the Lord.

When the doctrine of purgatory began to emerge and take shape, the primary emphasis was on sanctification. However, there was also another element present as well, and the Roman Catholic view of purgatory has always included this other dimension along with sanctification. This other element was the idea that purgatory is about satisfaction, which is the idea of undergoing punishment to satisfy the justice of God.[6]

So in short, the doctrine of purgatory can be understood in terms of sanctification, in terms of satisfaction, or in terms of some combination of the two. By the time of the Reformation, the emphasis on satisfaction had come to predominate over sanctification, and in much later Roman Catholic theology, the emphasis on satisfying the justice of God was the exclusive emphasis. So let's look at the satisfaction view of purgatory a little more carefully, since that is the view most Protestants probably think of when the doctrine is mentioned.

Satisfaction Alone . . .

The whole notion of satisfaction is integral to the Roman Catholic doctrine of penance, which has three parts. When sin has been committed, three things are required for things to be made fully right according to the Roman Catholic view. The first is contrition, which simply means the guilty person must be truly sorry and sincerely repent of what has been done. The second is confession, which is the requirement that the sin must be confessed to a priest.

The third part of penance is what is most crucial to understand, however, for our purposes. In addition to truly being sorry and confessing one's sin, the person must make satisfaction by accepting whatever punishment is imposed by the priest. That is necessary to satisfy the justice of God. Now if a person fails to make satisfaction, he or she must undergo the appropriate punishment in purgatory until God's justice is satisfied.

A classic statement of the view that purgatory is exclusively about satisfaction was written by French theologian Martin Jugie and published in English around the middle of the twentieth century after going through seven editions in French. Jugie's book is interesting because he claims simply to represent official Roman Catholic doctrine, and he cites classic sources to defend his claim. Let us consider three points he makes to underscore his claim that purgatory is entirely about satisfaction.

First, he distinguishes sharply between the concept of *purification* and that of *expiation*. The latter term is an important theological word that simply refers to the idea of making things right with someone who has been offended. Matters are made right when the offending party has undergone the necessary punishment to satisfy the demands of justice.

In Jugie's view, the soul is instantly purified the moment it leaves the body (a view similar to that of many Protestants). So purgatory is not needed as a matter of purification. Rather, it is entirely about satisfying justice. "In a word," Jugie sums up, "Purgatory must be looked on as a liquidation of the past, not as a march with face lifted towards the future, towards an ideal not yet attained."[7]

Second, Jugie holds that the length of time one spends in purgatory and the intensity of the suffering depend on the number and the seriousness of the sins for which satisfaction has not been made. One who has several serious sins to be dealt with has to undergo a longer and more intense period of punishment for God's justice to be satisfied.

Third, Jugie argues that the satisfaction view of purgatory makes the best sense of how indulgences work. If what is at stake is a debt that needs to be paid, then others can help us pay the debt, as long as it is paid. But if purgatory is about cleansing and purification, it makes no sense how anyone could do that for us or on our behalf. If I am dirty and need a bath, it will not do me any good for you to take a bath.

Crystalizing the Differences

Now the differences between these two ways of conceiving of the nature and purpose of purgatory are profound indeed.[8] Whereas the sanctification model is about moral and spiritual transformation, the satisfaction model is about exacting punishment to pay a debt of justice. Whereas the sanctification model looks forward to the goal of achieving spiritual perfection and holiness, the satisfaction model looks backward to a "liquidation of the past."

But perhaps the difference between the two models can be seen most clearly in the reason each believes purgatory requires a measure of time. Whereas the sanctification model believes achieving the goal of holiness is a pursuit that takes time to fully accomplish, the satisfaction model holds that the punishment of purgatory must be exactly as long and as intense as necessary to satisfy the demands of justice. Dorothy Sayers draws the contrast like this: "Purgatory is not a system of Divine book-keeping—so many years for so much sin—but a process of spiritual improvement which is completed precisely when it is complete."[9]

Now I reiterate, the satisfaction model of purgatory was in full force at the time of the Reformation and remained so for centuries after that. And it is certainly understandable why the

Reformers rejected the doctrine so passionately. Recall Calvin's question: "For what means this purgatory of theirs but that satisfaction for sins is paid by the souls of the dead after their death?" For the Reformers, purgatory represented nothing less than a denial that the death of Christ was sufficient to save us from the guilt of our sins and the punishment we deserve. Purgatory means we have to suffer to satisfy the justice of God.

And it was this view of purgatory that fueled the indulgence business to such spectacular heights. Recall the example above of Tetzel, who held out the specter of loved ones suffering terrible pain in purgatory, suffering that can be entirely eliminated "as soon as the coin in the coffer rings."

But here is the point I want to emphasize. To reject the satisfaction model of purgatory is not necessarily to reject the sanctification model. The sanctification model of purgatory offers an entirely different account of why we need purgatory. Indeed, the sanctification model of purgatory is entirely compatible with Protestant theology and, moreover, is an altogether natural fit in some versions of Protestant theology. Let us turn now to consider one very interesting example of how purgatory is affirmed by a highly regarded Protestant thinker and writer.

C. S. Lewis and Mere Purgatory

Near the end of his life, C. S. Lewis wrote a little book entitled *Letters to Malcolm*, in which he offered spiritual advice on prayer and other related matters. In one of the chapters, he discusses praying for the dead and endorses the practice, noting that many of the people he loved most had already died. One of those persons he no doubt had in mind was his wife, Joy, who had died of cancer a few years before. As Lewis reflected on this practice, he recognized that prayer for the dead suggested purgatory. For if the dead can benefit from our prayers, then that implies they are still making spiritual progress and still growing in grace. Lewis did not shrink from this implication and forthrightly declared, "I believe in purgatory."[10]

The fact that C. S. Lewis believed in purgatory is a matter of considerable significance. C. S. Lewis is in all probability the most influential Christian writer of the twentieth century, and his influence remains strong well into the twenty-first century. Moreover, although he was a Protestant, he had a unique gift for communicating "mere Christianity," the core doctrines of the faith that are shared by orthodox believers of all the great theological traditions.

But even more interesting for our present concerns is the fact that Lewis is an evangelical icon. Indeed, his writings are especially influential in evangelical Protestantism, particularly his most famous overtly theological book, *Mere Christianity*, which has perhaps shaped the movement more than any other single book outside the Bible.

So Lewis was a Protestant. Lewis believed in purgatory. Lewis is an evangelical icon. What I want to show now is that purgatory actually flows most naturally from those beliefs that Lewis identified as "mere Christianity." Insofar as Protestants can profess "mere Christianity" as a faithful expression of their theology, they have no reason to reject purgatory out of hand. Indeed, they have excellent reasons to affirm it, at least in the form that Lewis did.[11]

The Gift of Salvation

Let us begin with the most famous passage in *Mere Christianity*, namely, Lewis's famous argument for the deity of Jesus. His argument here is based on the extraordinary claims Jesus made for himself, such as his claim to forgive sins.

> A man who was merely a man and said the sort of things Jesus said would not be a great moral teacher. He would either be a lunatic—on a level with the man who says he's a poached egg—or

else he would be the Devil of Hell. You must make your choice. Either this man was, and is, the Son of God: or else a madman or something worse.[12]

This of course, is the Lord, liar, lunatic trilemma, and Lewis pushes his readers to conclude that Jesus is who he said he was, the Son of God incarnate, the Lord of the universe.

Now unfortunately, I think many readers of *Mere Christianity* have not paid sufficient attention to the rest of the book. What Lewis spells out in the remainder of the book, in short, is an explanation of what it means to believe Jesus is Lord. The trilemma is not just a clever apologetic argument with a striking conclusion. Rather, it is a conclusion with radical practical implications that will utterly transform our lives if we take it seriously.

In the very next chapter of the book, Lewis goes on to discuss how Jesus provides for our salvation. His conclusion that Christ is indeed who he claimed to be, the Son of God who has the right to forgive sins, leads him to explore the great Christian doctrine of the atonement. How exactly does Jesus's death and resurrection bring us salvation?

While Lewis provides an answer to this question, it is important to emphasize that he offers his theory of the atonement as nothing more than that, a theory. He certainly recognizes that the atonement itself is essential to Christianity but insists that a particular understanding of how it works is not.

But it is worth noting that he rejects the view that is probably the most popular among contemporary believers, the "penal substitutionary" theory of atonement. This is the view that Christ was punished in our place and thereby satisfied the justice and wrath of God, allowing us to be forgiven. He admits to finding this view morally implausible as well as "silly," though not as silly as he did before writing *Mere Christianity*.

Lewis's own theory of atonement is colored, naturally, by his understanding of the human predicament, of how our sin has affected our relationship with God. He describes fallen human beings as having gotten themselves into a big hole and needing some radical measures to get them out of it. The question is what sort of hole we are in.

As Lewis sees it, we have dug ourselves in by going our own way and acting as if we are independent beings who belong to ourselves. We are under the illusion that we can run our own lives and achieve happiness on our own terms. What this shows is we need some pretty drastic treatment if we are to be saved. We need far more than some sort of superficial remedies aimed merely at improving us or making us a little better than we are.

Lewis's conviction is that the only way out of this hole is by way of radical repentance, complete surrender. We need to get completely to the bottom of our problems; we need to be restored and remade "from the ground floor" up.[13] Getting clear on this is the key to understanding his view of the atonement.

In his view, the heart of the work of atonement is accomplished in the ironic role he ascribes to Christ when he calls him the "perfect penitent." The irony lies in the fact that a perfect person does not need to repent, but only such a person could "repent" perfectly. Since none of us are perfect, no merely human being could successfully pull off this project. And since God in his nature never has to surrender, suffer, and die, he does not seem suited to the task.

But here is where the incarnation of Jesus provides the solution to the problem. If God became man, Lewis points out, if he took on human nature, the resulting person could achieve what is needed. "He could surrender His will, and suffer and die, because He was man; and He could do it perfectly because He was God. You and I can go through this process only if God does it in us; but God can do it only if He becomes man."[14]

In surrendering his will, even to the point of death, Christ offered to God the perfect obedience that we owed to him. He gave the perfect "repentance," the complete apology, if you will,

that none of us could offer, and he thereby made good our defi-
ciency. "This is the sense in which he pays our debt, and suffers
for us what he himself need not suffer at all."[15]

Notice that the atonement so understood is still "substitutionary" in some sense, though not in the penal sense of Christ taking
our punishment. Rather, he is our substitute who surrenders his
will completely to God on behalf of all of us who have not.[16]

However, it is very important to be clear that Lewis does not
believe Christ is our substitute in the sense that we are now ex-
empt from perfect repentance since he did it on our behalf. Quite
to the contrary. Repentance is not an optional matter God can
dispense with, nor is it what God requires of us before he will
take us back. Rather, "it is simply a description of what going
back to him is like. If you ask God to take you back without
it, you are really asking him to let you go back without going
back. It cannot happen."[17]

Lewis's insistence on repentance as the very essence of what is
necessary for us to be saved is a different emphasis than we find
in many Protestant evangelicals. For many of them the heart of
the matter is justification by faith. In particular, justification is
understood to be God's gift to those who have faith in Christ's
atonement, typically understood in terms of penal substitution.
For those so justified, Christ's righteousness is "imputed" to
them so that God views them as righteous.[18]

By striking contrast, Lewis never once employs the term "justification" in *Mere Christianity*, nor does he ever suggest that
faith is a matter of having the righteousness of Christ imputed
to us. It is not the case in his view that those who have trusted in
Christ are viewed as righteous in such a way that all their sins,
past, present, and future, are covered by his blood. He certainly
believes that Christians who put their faith in Christ are justified in the sense that they are forgiven and accepted by God.
However, he does not subscribe to the notion of "justification
by faith" as the term is used by many evangelicals.[19]

It's All by Faith

Lewis does, however, clearly believe we are saved by grace, through faith alone. However, the faith through which we are saved is not a one-time act of belief that puts us right with God forever. Rather, it is an ongoing, dynamic relationship of trust and obedience in which we yield ourselves to God more and more until he fully fills our hearts and lives.

To put it another way, Lewis believes that we are being formed through our everyday choices into persons who have the sort of attitudes and desires that will, at the end of the day, make us at home either in heaven or in hell.

> And taking your life as a whole, with all your innumerable choices, all your life long you are slowly turning this central thing [the part of you that chooses] either into a heavenly creature or into a hellish creature: either into a creature that is in harmony with God, and with other creatures, and with itself, or else into one that is in a state of war and hatred with God, and with its fellow creatures, and with itself.[20]

There is nothing arbitrary or legalistic about who enters heaven and is finally saved, as Lewis sees it. Notice his emphasis on our "life as a whole" and our "innumerable choices" throughout our whole life. In these choices we are "slowly" being transformed into either a hellish or a heavenly creature. We cannot enter heaven if heaven has not first entered us and formed us in its image.

Lewis spells out his understanding of how this transformation is acquired through faith in a fair amount of detail in two chapters of *Mere Christianity*.[21] There he distinguishes between two levels of faith, the first of which is the familiar notion of taking as true the doctrines of Christianity. Faith in this sense is simply believing from the heart that Jesus is the Son of God, that he died for our sins, was raised from the dead, and so on. The second level of faith is less familiar but is particularly required by our need for radical transformation, as we shall see below.

Higher Faith for a Deeper Problem

Lewis carefully specifies what is distinctive about the second level of faith and why it is higher than the first one. Faith in this sense is higher, he says, because it cannot be exercised until a person has already gone some distance down the road on his or her way back to God. Traveling this road is a matter of moral effort, he explains, but, somewhat paradoxically, the effort we expend in this fashion will not get us to our goal. Rather, what this effort actually makes clear to us at the level of our personal experience is that we are incapable of living as God requires us to live.

As Lewis puts it later in his book, we discover a deeper problem underlying our acts of sin that need to be forgiven. "We begin to notice, besides our particular sinful acts, our sinfulness; begin to be alarmed not only at what we do, but about what we are."[22] Notice, the problem is much more serious than *what we do*. It ultimately comes down to *what we are*. And what we are needs more than forgiveness. It needs deep transformation. Only when there is a profound and thorough change in *what we are* will there be a consistent and lasting change in *what we do*.

Lewis illustrates with the example of a man who often loses his temper when he is provoked. The sudden provocation is not the cause of his losing his temper. It only exposes the fact that he has a problem in that regard. It is like the case when you quickly open the door of the cellar, and you see rats scurrying to hide. Your sudden opening of the door does not create the rats; it only exposes the fact that they were there all along.

Apparently the rats of resentment and vindictiveness are always there in the cellar of my soul. Now that cellar is out of reach of my conscious will. I can to some extent control my acts: I have no direct control over my temperament. And if (as I said before) what we are matters even more than what we do—if, indeed, what we do matters chiefly as evidence of what we are— then it follows that the change which I most need to undergo is a change that my own direct, voluntary efforts cannot bring about.[23]

Notice, we discover we need a change that we cannot bring about by our own "direct, voluntary efforts." We cannot, however, genuinely arrive at this realization without serious and sustained effort. We genuinely have to try to live up to God's standards, and try hard!

Only when we realize that we cannot root out the rats ourselves are we properly prepared to exercise faith in the second and higher sense that Lewis distinguishes. When we have reached this point, we are truly aware of our inability and therefore ready to trust God to do in us what we cannot do for ourselves.

To Dance with God, We Have to Be Like Jesus

Lewis identifies the nature of this faith more clearly in book 4 of *Mere Christianity*, where he elaborates most explicitly on Christ's intentions for us once we open ourselves to him and allow him to have his way with us. And notice, this final book is about the doctrine of the Trinity. The amazing truth that God is an eternal relationship of love in three persons is the ultimate basis of our salvation. Indeed, the very essence of salvation is a loving relationship that draws us into the fellowship of the three persons of the Trinity in order to share the joys and delights of being children of God.

Recall from chapter 1 that Lewis depicts this stunning reality in vibrant terms that are deeply appealing. In Christianity, he points out, "God is not a static thing—not even a person—but a dynamic, pulsating activity, a life, almost a kind of drama. Almost, if you will not think me irreverent, a kind of dance."[24] So for us to participate in this relationship, we must join the drama and take our place in the dance.

The problem, of course, is our sin—not just what we do but what we are. Our sin keeps us out of step with the trinitarian dance of love and joy. Salvation is not only about forgiving our acts of sin but also about changing us so we can join the dance. Becoming holy is like learning the trinitarian dance steps so well they become second nature. If we want to dance with God, we have to be like Jesus.

Lewis concludes the chapter by reiterating again what he takes to be the very center of the Christian enterprise. "Every Christian is to become a little Christ. The whole purpose of becoming a Christian is simply nothing else."[25] God wants to make us like Jesus so that we can enjoy the dance!

Seriously? God Wants to Make a Little Jesus Out of *Me*?

Now this extraordinary description of what God is up to can sound daunting and unrealistic. That each of us should become a "little Christ" may sound like a goal that is not only utterly out of reach for us but also very much at odds with the reality of who we are as we struggle with various sins, defects, petty resentments, and embarrassing weaknesses. Lewis is mindful of this and offers an encouraging description of how God's purpose for us goes forward in a matter as simple as saying our prayers.

Indeed, Christ himself is the agent of transformation who is remaking us in his image every time we encounter him. Lewis reminds us in very strong terms that Christ remains very much a living man, as much so as any one of us, and still as much God as he was before the world began. It is the very Son of God who is steadily at work in our lives, putting our old self to death and replacing it with a self like his, however slow and sporadic the progress may sometimes appear to be.[26]

As this remarkable reality sinks in, it must be utterly clear, Lewis insists, that Christ is singularly committed to finishing the job. While we may be satisfied with much less than he has in mind and gladly settle for something far short of what he is determined to accomplish in our lives, he will never be satisfied until our full transformation is complete. We should be under no illusion that he will settle for anything short of making us completely like himself. Christ was not talking "vague, idealistic gas" when he called his disciples to perfection.[27] He meant exactly what he said.

> That is why He warned people to "count the cost" before becoming Christians. "Make no mistake," He says, "if you let me, I will make you perfect. The moment you put yourself in My hands, that is what you are in for. Nothing less, or other, than that. You have free will, and if you choose, you can push Me away. But if you do not push Me away, understand that I am going to see the job through. Whatever suffering it may cost you in your earthly life, whatever inconceivable purification it may cost you after death, whatever it costs Me, I will never rest, nor let you rest, until you are literally perfect—until my Father can say without reservation that He is well pleased with you, as He said He was well pleased with me. This I can do and will do. But I will not do anything less."[28]

Although Christ is utterly committed to making us perfect, there is one possible obstacle he may not be able to overcome, namely, our freedom. While we do not have the ability to transform ourselves or to become perfect by our own power, we do have the ability to prevent him from making us so. We cannot bargain for less than perfection or call the shots if we want him to remain in our lives. We can, however, push him away and refuse to allow him to finish what he started, a point that Lewis goes on to reiterate several times.[29]

Notice also that the perfection Christ is determined to accomplish in our lives may cost us "inconceivable purification" after death. Lewis does not elaborate on this point here, but it is clear he thinks there will be postmortem work to be done in order to complete the project of our perfection. A few paragraphs after the long passage above, he repeats the striking vision of what God plans to do in our lives, insisting that nothing ever recorded of the greatest saints in terms of holiness or heroism is beyond what he finally intends to do in all of us.

Let that sink in. God wants to make all of us as holy as Saint Francis of Assisi, John Wesley, and Mother Teresa. But really, that is nothing compared to his ultimate goal of making us like Christ, his beloved Son with whom he is well pleased. We should not be discouraged when we realize how far short of that we often fall. "The job will not be completed in this life; but he means to get us as far as possible before death."[30]

It is apparent now, I take it, that the doctrine of purgatory is perfectly compatible with "mere Christianity." Indeed, it is not only compatible with it; it flows naturally out of those basic Christian truths as Lewis understood them. Let us now return to Lewis's explicit statement on purgatory in *Letters to Malcolm*.

Why Our Souls Demand Purgatory

Immediately after his forthright statement "I believe in Purgatory," Lewis made clear what view of the doctrine he was affirming. He began by noting that the Reformers had good reason to reject purgatory as it was understood during their time: "I don't mean merely the commercial scandal. If you turn from Dante's *Purgatorio* to the Sixteenth Century, you will be appalled by the degradation. . . . In fact, the very etymology of the word *purgatory* has dropped out of sight. . . . It is a place not of purification but purely of retributive punishment."[31] Notice also that Lewis

109

clearly distinguishes between what I have called the sanctification model (purification) and the satisfaction model (retributive justice) and that he affirms the former and repudiates the latter.

Lewis went on to spell out his understanding of what motivates purgatory, and it is radically different from what motivates the satisfaction view of purgatory.

> Our souls *demand* Purgatory, don't they? Would it not break the heart if God said to us, "It is true, my son, that your breath smells and your rags drip with mud and slime, but we are charitable here and no one will upbraid you for these things, nor draw away from you. Enter into joy"? Should we not reply, "With submission, sir, and if there is no objection, I'd *rather* be cleaned first." "It may hurt, you know"—"Even so, sir."[32]

As Lewis sees it, then, the demand for purgatory is not a demand for justice or punishment but rather the demand of love. It is the desire of the soul to be fully clean before entering the presence of a holy God.

Another way to think about Lewis's point here is to think about John Wesley's view of the relationship between holiness and happiness. Whereas we often tend to think of holiness as some sort of legalistic demand that God imposes upon us, Wesley saw it as the very key to happiness. In his view, the holier we are, the happier we will be, since there "is an inseparable connection between holiness and happiness."[33] So God's demand of holiness is not some stern, heavy-handed imposition but rather his passion for our happiness. And for us to aspire to holiness is to aspire to the happiness we can only find in a perfected relationship with a holy God.

Here it is worth noting an objection that is often raised to purgatory. Invariably when I discuss the doctrine, someone points out that the blood of Christ has paid for our sins, and we are therefore under no condemnation. We are saved by grace through faith alone, so the objection goes, so once our sins are under the blood, there is no need for purgatory to make us fully clean or to perfect our relationship with God.

Rooting Out Rats Requires More Than Forgiveness

Well, the objection that purgatory is superfluous since our sins are under the blood, though understandable, is wide of the mark. What is at issue here is not acts of sin we have done but rather what we are, as Lewis points out. Acts of sin can be forgiven and not in any way be held against us, but the issue of what we are—our sinful tendencies, those rats in the cellar—cannot simply be forgiven away. It needs a different kind of treatment, namely, the transformation of sanctification. And that transformation is just as much a matter of grace that we claim through faith as justification and forgiveness are.

Consider an analogy. Suppose a man has a serious problem with his temper, indeed so serious that he abuses his wife emotionally with the obvious result that their relationship often suffers. The problem is deeply rooted in his character due to a long history of poor choices and patterns of behavior. Suppose that despite this serious problem, his wife sincerely loves him and is willing to forgive him for his many failures and hurtful behaviors. Moreover, he also loves her and regrets it when he loses his temper and hurts her. He is often frustrated and disappointed by his own behavior.

In our analogy, his wife's forgiveness is like the grace of forgiveness and justification. But here is the point. For him to have the sort of truly loving relationship with his wife that God intends, he needs far more than forgiveness. He needs to have his character flaws repaired so that he can return the sort of love to his wife that she extends to him. And indeed, precisely for this reason, to the degree that he loves his wife and values their relationship, he will want to get his character issues resolved. And, for this very reason, he will deeply desire to undergo whatever healing and transformation he needs in order to remove the barriers that keep him from a truly healthy and satisfying relationship with his wife. To the degree that he loves his wife and wants a healthy relationship with her, he will "demand purgatory"!

A true relationship is a two-way street. For us to have the sort of loving relationship with God for which we were created, it is not enough that God loves us. We must return his love! And our sinful tendencies prevent our relationship from being what God desires it to be. Again, it is not enough to be forgiven or to have our sinful *acts* covered by the blood. We need that additional work of grace that transforms *who we are* in the depths of our being so that we can truly enjoy our relationship with the God of holy love.

The sort of help this man needs, moreover, will take time. It will require a process of coming to see the truth about himself, acknowledging his responsibility for how he formed his character traits and habits, and so on. He will need to see where he has gone wrong and how he can change his ways of thinking and his behavior. This is what is involved in that thoroughgoing repentance that Lewis talked about. Brett Salkeld puts it well in his comment that "it is hard to imagine repenting fully of something that one does not understand fully."[34] Such a process not only takes time, but it can be painful as well. The truth often hurts even as it heals.

A Zap or a Process?

In concluding this chapter, I return to the point I made earlier that all Christian theological systems have to account for how we become impeccable, how we achieve a settled character such that sin is no longer possible for us. The common Protestant answer is that we get this character at the moment of death when God zaps us and instantly perfects us. The answer given by advocates of the doctrine of purgatory is that God gives us this character as the final stage of sanctification, a process that is carried forward from beginning to end as we exercise faith in cooperation with his grace.

I believe there are good reasons for Protestants as well as Roman Catholics to prefer the second answer. In saying this, let me emphasize that this is by no means a reason to "return to Rome," as people sometimes suggest to me when I defend the doctrine. To the contrary, this should encourage Protestants to retrieve a version of the doctrine that is entirely compatible with "mere Christianity," one purged of those elements of satisfaction that have led to the distortion of the doctrine and the abuses for which it is famous.

In any case, whether one is inclined to accept the zap view or purgatory as a continuing process will depend on what one believes about a number of central issues. The first of these is the question of how seriously God takes our freedom in the whole process of salvation. Insofar as one believes that sanctification is nonnegotiable and that our free response of faith and cooperation is essential to our sanctification and final salvation, one will have grounds to think that the doctrine of purgatory makes theological sense.

Another and closely related issue is whether the sanctification process requires time. Since God sanctifies us by truth, does it necessarily take some degree of time to understand the truth about God and ourselves and to internalize that truth? Again, insofar as one believes that it takes time to understand and internalize the truth as God reveals it to us, one will be inclined to affirm the doctrine of purgatory.

It is worth emphasizing that it is a matter of broad consensus that we must cooperate in our sanctification. Indeed, the Calvinist critics of my book in the issue of *Credo* that I cited above make it clear that this is also true of the Reformed tradition. Chris Castaldo puts it like this: "Sanctification is a

113

gift for which God is ultimately responsible, but this does not preclude human cooperation. It is precisely because God is at work in us, both to will and to work for his good pleasure, that we continue to work out our salvation with fear and trembling (Phil. 2:12–13)."[35]

I could not agree more. But here is the question. If we must cooperate in our sanctification in this life, is that not a good reason to think that we must continue to do so after death? Again, the issue is whether both sanctification and our free cooperation in it are nonnegotiable.

The answer some critics of purgatory give to this question is that Scripture clearly teaches otherwise. These critics point to the example of the thief on the cross, who was promised by Christ that "today you will be with me in paradise" (Luke 23:39–43) and to passages such as 2 Corinthians 5:8 and Philippians 1:21–23, where Paul anticipates being in the presence of Christ immediately after he dies.

I do not see that these texts rule out purgatory. Indeed, the advocate of purgatory gladly affirms that we are in the presence of Christ when we die and that to be in his presence is better than to remain in this fallen world. But this hardly precludes the possibility that our sanctification process will continue in the intermediate state. Indeed, Paul wrote that we can be confident "that he who began a good work in you will carry it on to completion until the day of Christ Jesus" (Phil. 1:6). Notice, he says that Christ will carry it to completion not at the point of our death but "until the day of Christ Jesus." This suggests that Christ will carry on this good work in the intermediate state between death and the final judgment.

Indeed, being in the presence of Christ and seeing him with full clarity is essential to complete our sanctification. "But we know that when he appears, we shall be like him, for we shall see him as he is" (1 John 3:2). But again, seeing him with full clarity is not an instantaneous thing. Commenting on this verse,

John Polkinghorne has observed that "there is a hint of a salvific process, for we can scarcely suppose that Christ will be taken in at a glance."[36]

It is important to emphasize this point because it is sometimes suggested that this passage rules out purgatory. That is, it is claimed that Christ will instantly perfect all believers when he appears at his second coming. But as Polkinghorne's comment suggests, this reading is open to considerable doubt. In fact, the apostle's language here is open-ended with respect to the details of how Christ will appear to believers at his second coming. The text does not say that there will be a singular moment of his appearing in which all believers will see him with full clarity. Nor does it say that all will instantly be like him. John leaves these details uncertain.[37]

Again, Love Is the Key

In any case, whether purgatory happens in an instant, as most Protestants think, or at the end of a process, it is a gift of transforming love. The key to understanding purgatory, then, is the same as the key to understanding heaven and hell, namely, the love of God. *Heaven* is the joy of being at home in the presence of a God of perfect love. *Hell* is the misery of choosing persistently to resist that love. And *purgatory* is the transformation of our character as we open our hearts to that love.

So understood, purgatory is not a matter of human works or an alternative to salvation by grace. To the contrary, it *is* a form of grace. Again, to pit purgatory against grace is to totally misconstrue the doctrine understood in terms of sanctification.

And if purgatory is a postmortem process, perhaps it will be something like the experience of the disciples with Jesus on the Emmaus road shortly after his resurrection (Luke 24:13–35). Perhaps Jesus will open the Scriptures to us as he did to them and show us the truths we have yet to understand and fully embrace. Perhaps he will take us through the journey of our lives and let us see ourselves with utter honesty in the light of his holy love. And as the light of this truth penetrates more fully into our minds and hearts, perhaps our hearts will burn as if a fire is cleansing everything that falls short of the glory of God. And then perhaps he will appear to us with shining clarity as we simultaneously see that we have become like him.

But he will not then vanish from our sight. Rather, our joy will be complete, never again to disappear.

5

SAVING SOULS AND/OR BODIES

Personal Identity in the Afterlife

In order to have a sense of who we are, we have to have a
notion of how we have become, and of where we are going.

—Charles Taylor[1]

Among the most commonly asked questions about heaven
is whether we will know each other when we get there.
The answer, which will become even more apparent by the end
of this chapter, is that we will know each other better than we
ever have. For we will know not only ourselves but others with
a depth of understanding that far surpasses the insight and
knowledge we have in this life.

Let's begin to approach these issues by looking at one of the
most intriguing of Jesus's appearances to his disciples after his
resurrection—namely, the Emmaus road appearance, which I
mentioned at the end of the last chapter. Part of the fascination of this account is that those two disciples (not two of the

original twelve) were talking *to* Jesus *about* Jesus, not realizing with whom they were talking! They were sharing with him their grief and disappointment over Jesus's death: "We had hoped that he was the one who was going to redeem Israel" (Luke 24:21).

"We had hoped"! Those are among the saddest words that can be spoken in any language. They express the searing pain of a soaring expectation that has been brought down to earth and crushed. That is how the crucifixion of Jesus had affected the disciples.

To make matters even more interesting, they went on to share with Jesus the rumors they had heard about his resurrection and their doubts about them. (Surely Jesus had a hard time not laughing at this point!) During this whole conversation, they did not realize it was Jesus with whom they were talking until they stopped for the night and sat down to eat together. Then, just as they recognized him, he vanished from their sight!

Understandably, they were excited when they realized what had happened. They rushed back to Jerusalem to report to the eleven disciples that Jesus had appeared to them and that it was true that he was raised from the dead. Right as they were sharing this astounding news, Jesus himself appeared among them. But apparently it seemed just too good to be true, for the disciples still doubted what they were seeing. "They were startled and frightened, thinking they saw a ghost. He said to them, 'Why are you troubled, and why do doubts rise in your minds? Look at my hands and my feet. It is I myself! Touch me and see; a ghost does not have flesh and bones, as you see I have.' When he had said this, he showed them his hands and his feet" (Luke 24:37–40). The story that had begun with shattered hope was utterly reversed in its final outcome. After Jesus ascended to heaven, we read, "Then they worshiped him and returned to Jerusalem with great joy" (Luke 24:52).

There are lots of important lessons to be drawn from this text, but here is the one I want to focus on for now. The resurrection of Jesus shows us some things about what is involved in saving human beings when God's final work of redeeming his creation is complete. In particular, it shows that God will save human beings in a way that restores the full integrity of human nature. And this will include restoring human relationships that have been shattered by death.

This requires, even more fundamentally, that human beings will maintain their personal identity. Notice Jesus's emphatically reassuring words: "It is I myself." The relationship with Jesus that they thought was hopelessly lost was restored because Jesus himself was standing among them. The man who showed them his hands and feet was the same man who had walked and talked with them for three years and had been crucified just days before. Indeed, the fact that Jesus showed them his hands and feet as marks of identity is significant. "A ghost does not have flesh and bones, as you see I have."

Identity Questions and the Nature of Human Beings

The claim that the man who appears to the disciples is the same man who was crucified days earlier is a striking example of an identity claim. Claims of identity are commonplace; most of us take them for granted, but they do raise some interesting questions. For instance, does a thing have to be exactly identical at a later time as it was at an earlier time to be the "same" thing?

Here it is helpful to note the distinction philosophers make between *numerical* identity and *qualitative* identity. A thing can be numerically the same in the sense that it counts as one thing rather than two or more, even if it changes in some respects. Jesus's body, for instance, seemed to have powers after his resurrection that it did not have before. It could appear or vanish in an instant, which apparently it could not do before the resurrection. But it is still numerically one and the same body.

And, of course, in the case of our own bodies, they are constantly undergoing various changes. My body today is hardly the same as it was as a teenager or a toddler. Indeed, according to biologists, the molecules in my body are constantly changing, and every one of them is replaced every seven years or so. Yet there is still an important sense in which it is true that my body today is the same body I had seven years ago. There is continuity along with change, and my body today generates the changes it will undergo tomorrow.

These observations raise the question of how much change something can undergo and still be identical with what it was at an earlier time. This question becomes particularly acute when we think about the Christian doctrines of the afterlife. Death is one of the most dramatic changes any person can undergo. An even more dramatic change, however, is resurrection of our bodies, which we anticipate sometime in the future.

So the obvious question is this: How do the dead maintain identity between death and resurrection? Is it necessary to survive in some form between death and resurrection in order to maintain continuity? Is continuity necessary for identity? And if so, what kind of survival is necessary? "How much" of us would have to survive between death and resurrection in order to claim that the survivor is identical with the person before he died? Would it be enough, for instance, if only our personality survived, but not our memories?

Now these questions are closely related to the more fundamental question of just what a human being is. In traditional theology and philosophy, the dominant view is that a human being is an immaterial soul intimately united with a material body. This view is called dualism because of the claim that a living human being has a dual nature, both material and immaterial, both body and soul.

What is particularly interesting about dualism for our concerns is the claim that the soul can exist apart from the body.

This is a belief held by dualists ranging from Plato, the great Greek philosopher who was born 427 years before Christ, to Descartes, the father of modern philosophy, who was a Christian, to many contemporary dualists.

A variation on dualism is the view of Thomas Aquinas, who held that the soul is the "form" of the body. This is a rather difficult view to understand, and those who hold it sometimes deny that it is a form of dualism. But Aquinas agrees with the dualist view on the key point that the soul can exist without the body, so in that sense, it is a variation on dualism.

More recently, this dominant dualism has been challenged by the view that human beings simply *are* their bodies. This view is sometimes called monism, because it says a human being is made up of just one thing, a body. It is also sometimes called physicalism or materialism because it holds that human beings are entirely physical or material in their nature. There is no literal soul or mind that exists as an actual thing in the same way the body exists.

Somewhat surprisingly, physicalism has become popular in Christian circles in recent years despite the dominance of dualism in the history of theology. A number of Christian thinkers have argued that dualism is not the biblical view of human nature and that it was imported into Christian theology from Greek philosophy. As they see it, dualism is a distortion of the biblical view that tends to devalue the body.

Death and Identity

Now let's think about what death means for each of these views and about the problems that are raised for personal identity between death and resurrection. For dualists, death is the separation of the soul and the body. The body without the soul is no longer alive, but the soul can still remain in conscious existence. The question is whether the separated soul is still "identical"

121

in any way with the person who has died and no longer has a living body.

For the physicalist, the problem seems to be even worse. If you simply *are* your body, when your body dies and no longer functions or has conscious experience, then *you* no longer live or function and have conscious experience. And if that is the case, it seems you no longer exist and therefore have no continuing identity.

Before exploring this further, let's look at a fascinating passage in Dante's *Purgatorio* that bears on these issues. This passage occurs shortly after he has arrived on the island of purgatory after his tour through hell with Virgil, his guide. On the island is the mountain that represents purgatory proper, which he and Virgil will climb together. Before this happens, a boat arrives with the souls of one hundred people who have recently died and have been admitted to purgatory.

What makes this passage fascinating is the interaction between Dante, who has not yet died, and one of these souls. In particular, Dante still has his body, whereas these souls do not have human bodies. They are surprised to see someone in purgatory who has not yet died, and they surround Dante and Virgil. Dante describes the scene as follows.

> I saw one of those spirits moving forward
> in order to embrace me—his affection
> so great that I was moved to mime his welcome.
>
> O shades—in all except appearance—empty!
> Three times I clasped my hands behind him and
> as often brought them back against my chest.
>
> Dismay, I think, was painted on my face;
> at this, that shadow smiled as he withdrew;
> and I, still seeking him, again advanced.
>
> Gently, he said that I could now stand back;
> then I knew who he was, and I beseeched
> him to remain awhile and talk with me.[2]

As this conversation continues to unfold, we learn the identity of "who he was" who had greeted Dante so eagerly. It turns out that this is the soul of his good friend Casella. In the lines that follow, Casella says, "As I loved you when I was within my mortal flesh, so, freed [from his flesh], I love you."

Dualism and Identity after Death

This scenario captures some of the central reasons why dualists believe we can maintain our personal identity between death and resurrection. Notice a few things here. First, Casella recognizes Dante and moves to greet him before Dante realizes who he was. This suggests that Casella still retains not only his memory but also his emotions and feelings. He remembers his friendship with Dante and his love for his friend while he was in his "mortal flesh." Moreover, he still has those feelings for Dante.

Indeed, as the conversation proceeds, we learn that Casella used to sing songs for Dante that he very much enjoyed. He requests that Casella sing for him, and Casella responds by singing a song the first line of which was a line from one of Dante's poems. Dante says the song was so sweet that the memory of it remained with him thereafter.

It is difficult, however, to imagine how a soul without a human body could be recognized, let alone sing a song. Of course, Dante is using poetic and dramatic license here to convey this scene. But perhaps there is some way souls without bodies can communicate with each other. Maybe they communicate with something like telepathy.

In any case, if the human soul retains consciousness, memory, feeling, and even the ability to communicate, it makes sense of how the soul provides continuity of identity in the period between death and resurrection. Of course, there are limits here. These are dramatically portrayed in Dante's futile attempt to embrace Casella. Each time he does, it is like hugging the air, and his hands come back empty to his own chest. Clearly, there is not much satisfaction in hugging a soul without a human body. Hugs without bodies come up pretty empty.

So while Casella cannot enjoy a full human experience without his body, it is intelligible how his identity remains intact as he moves through purgatory. Only when his body is resurrected and reunited with his soul will he be fully human. But in the meantime, it makes sense to say Casella remains very much in existence and that he retains continuity with the man he was before he died.

Physicalism and Identity after Death

Let us turn now to consider the physicalist position on human nature. How can personal identity be maintained between death and resurrection if we are identical with our bodies?

Well, one option is to say that God will give us a body in the intermediate stage between death and resurrection. In order to maintain continuity with our body in this life, God might even split a cell from our body and use that to generate a new body for us. This would not be the same as our resurrection body, which will not be given until the end of the world. But it would be a body that would allow us to remain alive and retain our personal identity in "intermediate heaven" as we await the resurrection. Indeed, continuity would be maintained by the fact that this body was generated from a cell of the previous body.

Randy Alcorn, who is not a physicalist, notes that some texts in the New Testament may suggest that Christians will have bodies in the intermediate heaven. He points first to Paul's words in which he anticipates life after death: "Meanwhile we groan, longing to be clothed with our heavenly dwelling, because when we are clothed, we will not be found naked. For while we are in this tent, we groan and are burdened, because

124

we do not wish to be unclothed but to be clothed with our heavenly dwelling, so that what is mortal may be swallowed up by life" (2 Cor. 5:2–4).

Paul's anticipation that we will "be clothed with our heavenly dwelling" could be taken to mean that he expects to have a body. Alcorn also mentions the fact that the martyrs in heaven are depicted as wearing robes (Rev. 6:9–11). While this language could well be symbolic, it could indicate that the saints in intermediate heaven have bodies.

In any case, Alcorn takes the view that if there are such bodies, they are only temporary and are not our real bodies. They would not have any sort of continuity with our bodies in this life or with our resurrection bodies. Our resurrection bodies will have continuity with our bodies in this life, our real bodies. Intermediate bodies would just be placeholders, as it were, in the time between death and resurrection.[3]

Even with this qualification, the notion that we receive bodies immediately after death seems to lessen the force of death and, accordingly, the future resurrection. The dualist view that we are without our bodies during the intermediate period is arguably more true to the reality that death is the last enemy yet to be overcome (1 Cor. 15:26). Identity is sustained for the dualist, but in a form that is less than fully human since we are not embodied during the intermediate period.

But there is another option as well for physicalists. They can "bite the bullet" and simply insist that the gap in conscious existence between death and resurrection is not a problem for personal identity. They can point to the fact that some things are "gappy" or "gap inclusive" by nature. These things have gaps in their existence that do not in any way threaten their identity. Consider the World Series in baseball, for instance. There are gaps between the games when no one is playing and sometimes rain delays during games, but that does not pose a problem for anyone who understands the nature of the World Series.

Maybe human existence is something like this. Perhaps there is a gap in our existence between death and resurrection, but when our bodies are raised to life again, our personal identity will remain intact. Our life and identity will continue just as the World Series will continue throughout the whole series of games.

Defenders of the "gappy" view can also appeal to God's knowledge and power to support their case. God can preserve all the memories of each person, all of his or her character and personality traits and so on, and he can restore all these when he resurrects the person. In other words, when God resurrects a body, he also resurrects the memories, personality, and so on that go with that body.

Another variation worth mentioning here is one suggested by physicist and theologian John Polkinghorne. He rejects the dualist understanding of human persons but affirms a position that might be described as a contemporary version of the Thomist view that the soul is the form of the body. He suggests that we think of the soul as the "information bearing pattern" that organizes the physical matter in our bodies. This pattern is a dynamic thing in Polkinghorne's view, and it changes as we have new experiences, new insights, and memories.[4]

Polkinghorne's proposal is that God can preserve in his memory all the individual, personal patterns of all people who have died. Then he can use these patterns to resurrect people and restore all the memories, insights, and so on that were woven into their individual patterns during their life. Again, the idea is that personal identity is maintained by God's infinite knowledge and wisdom, even though there is apparently no conscious awareness between death and resurrection.

Purgatory Limits Our Options

While dualism of some variety has clearly been the dominant view in traditional theology, there is also a good case to be made that it is the view most compatible with the teaching of Scripture.[5] It also makes sense of how our personal identity can be sustained between death and resurrection, as well as in the resurrection itself. Moreover, it does not in any way weaken the significance of the future resurrection, as the view that we will have bodies in the intermediate state arguably does.

Still, I would grant that all these views can make sense of how our personal identity can be sustained through death and resurrection. Questions can be raised about all of them; still, all of them appear to provide an account that is sufficient for personal identity in the life to come.

It is worth noting, however, that the "gappy" or "gap-inclusive" view does pose problems for the doctrine of purgatory. The reason is that purgatory is thought to occur after death in the intermediate period before the final resurrection.

In other words, the doctrine of purgatory assumes continued conscious survival between death and resurrection. Moreover, it assumes that the persons who survive retain their memory, their ability to think and make moral progress, and so on. So those who are inclined to accept this doctrine should accept either some version of dualism or some account of embodied existence between death and resurrection.

Adding Color to the Story

The discussion of personal identity so far may seem rather abstract, perhaps even impersonal in some ways. After all, it might be objected, you don't really get to know a person—who someone really is—by talking about the fact that he or she has a unique soul that can sustain conscious existence between death and resurrection. Nor do you do so by talking about that person's distinctive DNA or the form of his or her body that could be re-embodied.

Physical or metaphysical facts like these do not begin to tell the story of who a person really is in the sense we find most interesting. To tell *that* story, what we need is exactly that: a story!

Consider, for instance, this passage from Nicholas Wolterstorff, commenting on his son, Eric, who was tragically killed in a mountain-climbing accident.

> A center, like no other, of memory and hope and knowledge and affection which once inhabited the world is gone. Only a gap remains. A perspective on this world unique in this world which once moved about within this world has been rubbed out. Only a void is left. There's nobody now who saw just what he saw, knows what he knew, remembers what he remembered, loves what he loved. A person, an irreplaceable person, is gone. Never again will anyone apprehend the world quite the way he did.[6]

"Only a gap remains"! This line takes on additional poignancy when we are talking about a specific person and not a metaphysical theory of identity.

I had the privilege one time of meeting Eric while we were both graduate students at Yale. But I only met him. I never really got to know him. I never heard him share his most wonderful or most painful memories. I never got to hear him talk in depth about what he loved or his most cherished hopes. I never heard his story or how it shaped his unique perspective on the world.

But that is what is required to really know who a person is. That is what it takes to know someone as the truly irreplaceable person that he or she is and who fills a gap no one else can fill. So let's turn to look more carefully at this way of thinking about personal identity.

One philosopher who has explored this in detail is Charles Taylor, whose book *Sources of the Self* is one of the greatest philosophical books written in the past several decades. Taylor argues that there is an essential link between personal identity and one's orientation in what he calls "moral space." In a very important sense *who we are* is very much determined by *where we are* in relation to fundamental questions of value. Our deepest identity is revealed by what we think is good or bad, what is really worth doing and what is not, what is deeply meaningful and important and what is only trivial.

Being oriented in moral space is very much like being oriented in physical space. To be oriented in physical space is to know where you are, how you got there, and the important landmarks along the way. Taylor gives the example of a person who walks out of a drugstore in Montreal and turns the corner to see something that looks like the Taj Mahal staring him in the face. If he is properly oriented in physical space, he will not think that he is actually in India at that moment and viewing that famous structure. Rather, he will think that someone must be shooting a movie and that the "Taj Mahal" is part of the set.

The point is that you can't get to the Taj Mahal simply by turning a corner in the middle of Montreal. If you want to arrive at the real Taj Mahal, you must travel in the correct direction for the necessary distance to get there.

The same is true of moral space. To arrive at the moral destination we seek, we must travel in the right direction and cover the necessary distance required. In other words, authentic character is achieved by a journey that takes time as well as proper direction.

> It is not only that I need time and many incidents to sort out what is relatively fixed and stable in my character, temperament and desires from what is variable and changing, though that is true. It is also that as a being who grows and becomes I can only know myself through the history of my maturations and regressions, overcomings and defeats. My self-understanding necessarily has temporal depth and incorporates narrative.[7]

Notice, there is a history of our maturations, regressions, and so on, and we need to know our history to know ourselves. Anyone else who wants to know our true identity needs to know this history too. Who we are is disclosed in an ongoing story as we make our way through moral space.

Taylor makes the point about identity in terms of moral philosophy, but the same sort of point has been made by other thinkers in more directly theological terms. Consider these words from Joseph Ratzinger, later Pope Benedict XVI.

> Man is a temporal traveler along the way of knowing and loving, of decaying and maturing. His specific temporality also derives from his relationality—from the fact that he becomes himself only in being with others and being toward others. Entering upon love, or indeed refusing love, binds one to another person and so to the temporality of that person, his "before" and "after." The fabric of shared humanity is the fabric of shared temporality.[8]

Notice again, "man becomes himself only in being with others and toward others." Our personal identity is not a Lone Ranger sort of thing. Rather, who we are in terms of our character unfolds over time in relationship with others. Our moral and spiritual identity is very much forged by the history of our loving relationships, even if that includes the choice of refusing love or abusing it.

Let us consider one final example of this line of thought. Theologian Colin Gunton, drawing on the doctrine of the Trinity, also argues that our individual identity is finally a relational matter. It should not surprise us that our particular identity is relational since the identity of the divine persons in the Trinity is also relational. The Son of God, for instance, has his particular identity as the Son because of how he is related to the Father. The same basic point applies to us: "All particulars are formed by their relationship to God the creator and redeemer, and to each other. Their particular being is a being in relation, each distinct and unique and yet inseparably bound up with the other, and ultimately all, particulars."[9]

This comment from Gunton brings into focus the heart of our true identity. Who we are is formed by our relationship to God and to each other. My identity is "inseparably bound up" with other persons as I relate to them, most of all to God himself.

Now let us summarize the key points from these thinkers. Who we are can be known fully only by knowing the story of our lives. At the heart of our story is what we love, what is important to us, and so on. The truth about us in this regard emerges in time as we form a stable character through many choices and experiences. Moreover, we are not alone in the journey of life. Rather, who we are and what we love and care about is very much revealed in our relationships, first with God and then with other persons as well. Our unique moral and spiritual identity is determined by the history of our choice to love God or not, as well as our fellow human beings. And that history continues to be written every day of our lives.

Losing Our Story, Losing Our Identity

It is worth highlighting that it was during the so-called Enlightenment that a number of philosophers began to reject the idea of personal identity. During this period of history, more and more intellectuals began to reject belief in God and the Christian faith and to rely solely on the powers of human reason to make sense of our lives. One of the most famous of these is David Hume, who argued that there is no real basis of continuity that makes me the same person today as I was a year ago or even a week ago. There is no real "self" in his view, just a series of experiences that have no underlying unity.

As Alasdair MacIntyre points out, it is not surprising that the problem of personal identity was generated in the aftermath of rejecting the Christian story. In particular, MacIntyre points out that in rejecting the Christian story, many people lost belief in "life-long accountability and in the teleological ordering of each life."[10]

Think about the importance of those two fundamental beliefs and what it means when they are lost. To lose belief in "life-long accountability" undermines the conviction that there is a deep unity to our life as a whole. To lose the idea of a "teleological ordering" is to lose the vision that there is an "end" or a purpose of life toward which we should aim. What this suggests is that in losing the Christian story, many people lost confidence in the idea that their own personal story has deep meaning and significance.

It is striking in this connection to note that Nietzsche roundly rejected what he called "the error of free will" and, with it, the idea of accountability. Nietzsche wrote, "We deny God; in denying God, we deny accountability; only by doing *that* do we redeem the world."[11] Nietzsche's "redemption" is not a matter of forgiveness and moral transformation under accountability to a God of holy love. Rather, redemption for him is a denial of God and any sort of accountability for our choices or our lives as a whole.

The Christian story, with the prospect of heaven and hell before us, is a powerful vision of "life-long accountability" and "the teleological ordering of each life." We must all appear before the judgment seat of Christ to account for how we have lived and the choices we have made. Moreover, there is a true "end" to our lives, a true *telos* toward which we should be striving in the journey of life. That *telos* is an end of incomparable beauty and goodness, as we saw in the first chapter. To achieve that end is nothing less than eternal joy, whereas to miss it is eternal misery.

Heaven and hell, then, are vital resources for personal identity. They provide direction as we navigate moral space, and they define for us the ultimate good we should seek and the evil we should avoid. They tutor us on what we should love, what we should care about, and the choices we should make. And as all of this is sorted out for us as our story unfolds, our true identity becomes ever more apparent.

Purgatory and the Preservation of Identity

The doctrine of purgatory also has a distinct contribution to make to personal identity. The argument for this claim was developed several years ago by David Brown as one of a series of three interrelated arguments in favor of purgatory. The starting point for his argument is the assumption that we can know and identify ourselves "only through continuity with the past."

Simply put, the only way I can know who I am in the present is by knowing my past as well. In particular, I must understand the connection between my past and my present. How did my present grow or develop out of my past? If I cannot answer this, I do not really know who I am now.

The key premise of his argument, however, is the following: "Therefore, the more dramatic the contrast in character between a person A at time x and person B at subsequent time y, the more likely is the latter individual B to doubt whether he could in fact be the same person as person A at time x."[12] Simply put, if I am dramatically different today from a person I remember from yesterday, I would rightly wonder if I was that person from yesterday.

Here is where purgatory comes in. Most of us are not perfect now, nor will we be when we die, but we will be perfect in heaven. So what we need is an account of how such imperfect people can be transformed in a way that preserves their identity. Such change must be gradual enough and intelligible enough that continuity is maintained with our past as we grow toward perfection and actually achieve it.

To get a better handle on this, consider this thought experiment that Brown offers in defense of his argument. Imagine that someone wakes up in your bed who looks like you, talks like you, and has your memories, but is quite different from you in one important respect: he is completely morally perfect. The lousy attitudes, character flaws, resentments, petty jealousies,

133

and so on that you had when you went to bed the previous night are nowhere to be seen in this person. He is literally a perfect saint, and he claims to be you. If this person woke up in your bed, would you not doubt that this person was really "you"?

Let's reflect some more on this thought experiment by considering a famous character from literature, namely, Ebenezer Scrooge. He is a famous case of a man who went to bed one night as a very nasty man and woke up the next day as an awesome guy you would love to have as a friend. The heart of the story, of course, is about how that dramatic change occurred.

Let us alter the story, however, so that he is not visited by the ghost of his dead friend Jacob Marley or by the Ghost of Christmas Past and the other two spirits. Let us say instead that he goes to bed that night remembering the events of the day with a smug sense of self-satisfaction. He remembers how his nephew visited him and invited him to Christmas dinner, and how he mocked the whole idea of Christmas, brushing off the invitation with his characteristic line, "Bah, humbug."

Next he remembers poor, miserable Cratchit, shivering in the cold as he toiled away at his monotonous job and then meekly asking if he might have Christmas Day off. Scrooge chuckles at Cratchit's subservient attitude and how he cowers under his threats.

Then he recalls the pleasure with which he dispatched the idealistic dreamers who were trying to raise money for the poor to relieve their needs at Christmas. He takes particular delight in his own retort when told the poor would rather die than go to the prisons and workhouses: "If they would rather die, they had better do it, and decrease the surplus population."[13] Laughing at his own cleverness, Scrooge falls peacefully asleep after repeating one more time, "Christmas! Bah, humbug."

The next morning when he awakens, he is feeling giddy and begins to think about his nephew's invitation to Christmas dinner. As he thinks about him, he has very affectionate feelings for him and decides he will surprise his nephew by showing up for dinner, bringing along gifts for him and his newlywed wife. The thought of this fills him with excitement and a sense of slightly mischievous pleasure.

Then he sits down for his morning tea, and over a cup of steaming Assam he begins to think about Cratchit. He notices that he also has warm feelings for him, along with a tender concern for his little son, Tiny Tim. As he savors his tea, he decides to surprise Cratchit with a promotion and to double his salary.

He then shares with his maid that he plans to attend Christmas dinner at his nephew's house. He goes on to tell her how fond he is of his nephew and how much he looks like his deceased mother, Scrooge's sister. He then orders the maid to take the rest of the week off, giving her a generous gift of money along with a raise. She is utterly stunned and leaves the house in a hurry, convinced that Scrooge has finally lost his mind.

But even more to the point, Scrooge himself is utterly baffled at his own thoughts and behavior. He remembers his actions and attitudes of the previous day and, indeed, many similar thoughts and actions over the past several years. As he reflects on these memories, he cannot fathom what has happened to him so that he now thinks and feels so radically different than he did just the day before. "Who am I?" he asks himself with true bewilderment, looking in the mirror as he dresses for Christmas dinner.

Sorry, Scrooge, No Getting Around the Process

Now it is obvious that to alter the story in this way totally destroys its integrity. Such dramatic change would leave readers as bewildered as it would Scrooge and his maid. The power and beauty of the story is due to the account of *how* Scrooge undergoes his radical transformation. The reason the story appeals to us is that it makes not only dramatic but psychological and moral sense of how the most despised man in town "became as good a friend, as good a master, and as good a man, as the good old city knew."[14]

Notice, he "became" as good a friend, master, and man as the old city ever knew. This implies that even after his encounter with the three ghosts, he still had some "becoming" to do. But for now the point is that if he woke up radically different from the way he was the night before, with no sense of continuity, no realistic sense of how that happened, he would not even know himself. He would face a serious identity crisis.

The point for emphasis here is that Dickens's account of Scrooge's initial transformation is presented as a process. Indeed, Scrooge gets a tour of his whole life, including his future yet to come. He gets to see how he had "become" the sort of man that he was and how his life would end up if he did not change. He has the chance to review the crucial choices he made by which he came to love money more than people. For instance, he witnesses the scene when he broke his engagement to his fiancée, who deeply loved him, because he had become more interested in getting rich than in developing loving relationships.

As he revisits these crucial episodes, he begins to see things in a completely different light; as a result, his hard heart begins to soften. One of the most telling of these scenes occurs during his visit from the Ghost of Christmas Present, who takes him to observe the Cratchit family Christmas dinner. As he observes this struggling family, he begins to feel love and compassion, especially for Tiny Tim. When the spirit tells him that Tiny Tim will die unless things change, Scrooge feels a concern he has never felt before. The spirit then reminds him of his earlier callous words about the "surplus population" and cautions him not to speak "until you have discovered What the surplus is, and Where it is. Will you decide what men shall live, what men shall die? It may be that in the sight of Heaven, you are more worthless and less fit to live than millions like this poor man's child."[15]

Notice particularly that Scrooge's self-centered perspective is challenged by appealing to "the sight of Heaven." Seeing things from that angle radically alters Scrooge's entire field of vision. He begins to see others, as well as himself, in a completely new light.

Of course, in reality, such a thorough reassessment of one's entire life could hardly happen in a night. But the point is that Dickens presents Scrooge's transformation as the result of a deep repentance that goes all the way to the roots of who he is and how he has become the person that he is. His transformation happens in stages, beginning with the insights he gains from the Ghost of Christmas Past all the way through the truth he learns from the Ghost of Christmas Yet to Come.

The suggestion here is that there are several layers in Scrooge's selfish character, and it is necessary to deal with each of these layers one at a time. There is no shortcut to the process necessary for deep change in his life.

Indeed, it is both amusing and telling to note that when he is visited by Marley, who foretells the visit of the three spirits, Scrooge is less than enthusiastic about the whole ordeal. Trying to be helpful, he proposes an abbreviated sort of process. "'Couldn't I take 'em all at once, and have it over, Jacob?' hinted Scrooge."[16]

Here it is worth noting that it is sometimes suggested that we can take a shortcut to sanctification by getting a new body. Once we leave these bodies behind, all our sins will be left behind as well, so it is claimed. The problem with this suggestion, however, is that it does not properly locate where our sin really lies. It does not identify where sin has its real stronghold. Sin does not reside primarily in our bodies but rather in our will, thoughts, attitudes, and so on.

The problem, in other words, is our heart, not simply our body. Jesus made this clear when he taught us that what makes us unclean is what comes out of our heart, what comes from within. That is the source of greed, malice, arrogance, folly, and so on (Mark 7:20–23).

Suppose Scrooge was given a new body, but nothing else changed. Well, if that were the case, he would simply be a man with a nasty heart and a great new body. Indeed, perhaps his new body would even give him one more reason to feel superior and look down on others less fortunate. Scrooge's problems lay in who he was within, in his way of thinking, in his values, and in his attitude toward other people. These elements are what shaped his character, not simply his body. Without a thorough overhaul of his character, without a new heart, a new body would not help him.

It Ain't Over 'til It's Over

It's tempting to agree with Scrooge's suggestion and just want to "have it over." The rest of the story, however, shows why this suggestion is misguided. For the story to have integrity, to have true unity and come to a satisfying resolution, it must play out until it reaches its proper end.

Pope Benedict XVI offered a highly suggestive definition of soul in one short line: "Soul is nothing other than man's capacity for relatedness with truth, with love eternal."[17] To be properly related to love eternal, we must come to terms with the truth, both about God and about other people, including ourselves. As we come to terms with truth and let love eternal have his way in our lives, we experience fully the salvation of our souls.

To put it another way, the more deeply we understand the Christian story of love eternal—the story of Trinity, incarnation, and resurrection—the more deeply we will understand our own story. And thereby we will fully come to know who we are.

WIPING AWAY EVERY TEAR?

The Afterlife and the Problem of Evil

My . . . intuitions are that the very worst evils are the ones that demand the most to be defeated and that Divine *goodness* to created persons cannot be sustained if God permits horrors beyond the reach of Divine defeat.

—Marilyn McCord Adams[1]

One of the most deeply stirring descriptions of what we can anticipate will happen when heaven comes to earth and God makes his home with his children is that "he will wipe every tear from their eyes. There will be no more death or mourning or crying or pain, for the old order of things has passed away" (Rev. 21:4).

But this very promise brings home to us the reality that we look forward to this day through eyes that are often filled with tears. With brutal regularity, we are reminded that the old order of things is still very much in force. The last enemy is still on the loose and wreaking havoc. Every day countless tears are shed over loved ones lost and relationships torn asunder as our last enemy strikes down ever more victims.

The shadow of death lurks everywhere and is not absent even in our greatest moments of joy and celebration. As couples enter into marriage, along with their hopes for a lifetime of love and joy comes the solemn reminder that even the most blessed marital unions last only "'til death us do part." Parents give birth to children knowing that in the course of time, their children will eventually bury them, or worse, they will bury their children.

But death is far from the only thing that produces tears in our world. There are all sorts of pain and suffering that leave their victims alive but still take an enormous toll in other ways. Those who suffer these forms of hurt are left not only with grief, regret, heartache, and shattering emotional or psychological damage, but also often with severe physical injury as well.

Moreover, death and suffering often come to people in ways that are so unspeakably outrageous that we wonder how matters could ever be made right in their lives again. Even if the day comes when "death will be no more," that may not be enough to rectify these outrages. The suffering that some people have undergone may be so extreme that nothing can ever fix or make up for it.

Indeed, one of the most famous objections to the doctrine of heaven in modern literature is a moral objection along these very lines. This objection is articulated with searing intensity by the character named Ivan in Dostoevsky's classic novel *The Brothers Karamazov*. Ivan paints the problem of evil in vivid colors in a conversation with his brother Alyosha, a pious monk. He brings the problem into razor-sharp focus by zeroing in on a particularly distressing aspect of the problem, namely, the suffering of little children. He builds his case by telling story after story of horrific cruelty to children at the hands of heartless adults. Each story he tells is like another punch in the gut.

Ivan brings his speech to a climax with a painfully graphic description of two such cases of cruelty. The first of these involved the heart-wrenching abuse of a little five-year-old girl by her well-bred, educated parents. This child was beaten and kicked by her parents until her whole body was one large bruise. Then to punish her further for not asking to get up in the middle of the night to go to the bathroom, they locked her in the freezing cold in the outhouse and smeared her face with her own excrement and forced her to eat it. He pictures this little girl vainly beating her fist against her chest and weeping as she prays to God to protect her.

The second story was about a small peasant boy who threw a rock while playing and accidentally hurt the paw of a hunting dog that belonged to a wealthy and powerful retired general. To make an example of the boy and to demonstrate his power over his subjects, he ordered the boy stripped naked and then commanded him to run. Then he set loose a pack of his hunting dogs, which ran him down and tore him to pieces as his mother was forced to watch.

Now all of us can agree that incidents like this are mind-numbing and heart-sickening. And for many people, such incidents are so terrible that the only honest conclusion they can draw is that there is no God, at least not a God who is perfectly good and all-powerful.

But the point for emphasis now is that Ivan insists that some evils are so monstrously bad that they cannot be fixed, even if there is a God. There is no sort of heaven, no final outcome, no ultimate "harmony" that could suffice to resolve these horrible outrages. Listen to his passionate protest against heaven on behalf of the children who have suffered such treacherous cruelty.

It is not worth one little tear of even that one tormented child who beat her chest with her little fist and prayed to "dear God" in a stinking outhouse with her unredeemed tears! Not worth it because her tears remain unredeemed. They must be redeemed, otherwise there can be no harmony. But how, how will you redeem them? Is it possible? . . . I do not, finally, want the mother to embrace the tormentor who let his dogs tear her son to pieces! She dare not forgive him! Let her forgive him for herself, if she wants to, let her forgive the tormentor her immeasurable maternal suffering; but she has no right to forgive the suffering of her child who was torn to pieces, she dare not forgive the tormentor, even if the child were to forgive him! And if that is so, if they dare not forgive, then where is the harmony? Is there in the whole world a being who could and would have the right to forgive? I don't want harmony, for the love of mankind I don't want it.[2]

As Ivan sees it, then, this earth is soaked with unredeemed tears, and this brutal reality undermines the deeply stirring promise that God will wipe every tear from our eyes. Many evils that have been committed are so grievous that they cannot be forgiven. And this means that some relationships are simply beyond restoration, even if death can be overcome.

Notice, moreover, that Ivan registers this protest on behalf of the victims of horrific suffering. It is, he claims, precisely his love for humanity that moves him to reject the prospect of heaven and to resign himself to the despair of hopeless moral indignation.

Sadly, the sort of scenarios Ivan describes have been repeated far more times than we are even aware. Countless persons, many of them children, have suffered unspeakable horrors in utter obscurity without anyone ever knowing about it or even paying them the minimal respect of regret. Reflecting on this painful reality only intensifies the force of Ivan's protest.

Such tragedies are not, however, confined to the pages of classic literature or to extreme upheavals in the lives of anonymous persons who may live halfway around the world. Indeed, many of us may be personally acquainted with persons whose lives have been ripped asunder by some sort of unspeakable tragedy.

I had a student several years ago for whose family this was the case. My student's sister, sixteen-year-old Suzi Holliman, was home from school one day with the flu. On that day, Ricky Lee Sanderson broke into the house to burglarize it with the intention of getting money to buy drugs. When he discovered Suzi at home, he raped her and then locked her in the trunk of his car, having decided to kill her. While he dug her grave, she was scratching on the closed lid of the trunk, desperately attempting to escape the terrible fate that she no doubt realized awaited her. After digging the grave, he strangled and stabbed her to death.

Shortly after the murder, Sanderson was arrested and pled guilty to charges of kidnapping and murder. He was sentenced to death two years after the crime. But the story does not end here.

Sanderson was converted after he was imprisoned and became an outspoken Christian in the years leading up to his execution. He later refused further appeals and requested the death sentence to be carried out because he claimed to be concerned that additional trials would cause further suffering for the Holliman family. When he finally went to his death thirteen years after the murder, he professed to be at peace and even said that he was prepared to meet his victim in the afterlife. "I think about facing Suzi Holliman when I'm executed. What's that going to be like? I'm ready to do it. I'm going to be with Christ."[3]

Understandably, Suzi's father was skeptical of Sanderson's conversion. Indeed, he could relate to at least part of Ivan's protest, despite the fact that he is a practicing Christian. Hugh Holliman was gut-wrenchingly honest about his own conflicted feelings for the man who ruthlessly murdered his daughter but later professed to be a fellow disciple of Christ who looked forward to meeting her in heaven. "The hopes and dreams he took away from us and the world—I tried but I can't forgive him. You know there is forgiveness there, but I can't see God totally forgiving him for something like that."[4]

Ivan Karamazov and Hugh Holliman raise hard questions. Let's face it, the Christian notion that heaven will wipe away all tears is a staggering thought. If heaven is real, no doubt there are many rapists, murderers, and terrorists who will be there along with their victims. Is this idealistic nonsense? Is it a moral absurdity? Or is it a profoundly moral hope?

Who Has the Moral High Ground?

Let's begin to explore answers to these questions by asking who has the moral high ground in this debate. Atheists who reject belief in God because of the problem of evil often claim the moral high ground in doing so. It is precisely their moral convictions that will not allow them to believe in a perfectly good, all-powerful God in the face of horrendous evil. Ivan, recall, registers his protest on behalf of humanity. It is his love for humankind that will not allow him to believe in a heaven that could redeem even the tears of those little children who have suffered such vicious cruelty.

The claim that atheists have the moral high ground here is far from apparent, however. While we can all agree on the feeling of outrage in the face of horrendous evil, it may call forth an altogether different sort of response than that represented by Ivan. Peter van Inwagen, for instance, says he has "never had the least tendency to react to the evils of the world by saying, 'How could there be a loving God who allows these things?' My immediate emotional reaction has rather been: 'There *must* be a God who will wipe away every tear; there *must* be a God who will repay.'"[5]

Of course, emotional reactions don't settle the truth question here one way or the other. It is still worth underscoring, however, that horrific evil may elicit the conviction that there *must* be a God who will make things right, just as it may call forth the conviction that there *cannot* be such a God.

Indeed, there is a further point to be made. It is arguable that if one is truly concerned for the suffering of innocent victims, then one should at least *hope* that there is a God and an afterlife that can set things right rather than rejecting that hope as Ivan does. Richard Creel puts the point as follows:

> Why hope that there is a God? Because of compassion for those who have suffered innocently; because of desire that their suffering not have been useless and terminal, i.e., redeemable after death. As long as it is logically possible that evil be defeated, that innocent suffering is not meaningless and final, it seems to me that we have a moral obligation to hope that that possibility is actual. Therefore we have a moral obligation to hope that there is a God because, if there is a God, then innocent suffering is not meaningless or final.[6]

Notice, Ivan's protest "for the love of mankind" has the ironic effect of writing off the sufferings of the very people he claims to be concerned about. His protest that rejects the hope of heaven means that their suffering is utterly meaningless and final. It is a permanent loss that can never be redeemed. The little boy who died in terror as he was torn to pieces is at best a monument to the absurdity of life. His dying cries will go unanswered by an indifferent universe, and he will never be heard from again.

Moreover, Ivan consigns to oblivion all the innocent sufferers we have never heard about. Again, their lives represent futile cries that go unheard and tears that fall to the ground with no one to ever know or care.

So despite Ivan's claim to the moral high ground, his position has less concern for the victims of terrible evil than it may first appear. It is precisely for "the love of mankind" that we have a moral obligation to hope that God exists and that heaven can redeem even the worst of evils.

How in the Name of Heaven Can All Tears Be Wiped Away?

The apostle Paul laid down for us the basic principle we need to answer this question: "I consider that the sufferings of this present time are not worth comparing with the glory about to be revealed to us" (Rom. 8:18 NRSV). Paul's claim here is that there is a glory we have yet to experience that utterly defies comparison with any suffering of this present time. Elsewhere, in a similar vein he wrote, "For this slight momentary affliction is preparing us for an eternal weight of glory beyond all measure" (2 Cor. 4:17).

When you read this phrase describing the suffering of this life as "slight momentary affliction," it might be tempting to dismiss Paul as a Pollyanna or a relatively sheltered guy who was insufficiently acquainted with the harsher side of reality. This charge, however, will not stick. Later in the book of 2 Corinthians, Paul catalogs the numerous sufferings he underwent in addition to several floggings, imprisonments, and brushes with death.

> Five times I have received from the Jews the forty lashes minus one. Three times I was beaten with rods. Once I received a stoning. Three times I was shipwrecked; for a night and a day I was adrift at sea; on frequent journeys, in danger from rivers, danger from bandits, danger from my own people, danger from Gentiles, danger in the city, danger in the wilderness, danger at sea, danger from false brothers and sisters, in toil and hardship, through many a sleepless night, hungry and thirsty, often without food, cold and naked. (2 Cor. 11:24–27 NRSV)

This gets my attention. Paul has clearly earned the right to talk about suffering. He is not the sort of guy whose idea of adversity was losing his iPhone (or whatever the first-century equivalent of that was). He lived, moreover, at a time when people who were accused of serious crimes were punished with crucifixion. He had a realistic measure of how bad suffering can be, but he still considered it "slight momentary affliction" compared to what God is preparing for us. Indeed, I think this phrase is one of the most suggestive in the whole New Testament when we take into account Paul's personal experience of suffering.

Marilyn McCord Adams has developed this idea of an immeasurable good as an essential component of a satisfactory Christian response to the problem of evil. It is simply fundamental to Christian theism that an intimate relationship with God is the greatest possible good; indeed, it is the one thing most essential to happiness and satisfaction.

Recall our discussion in chapter 1 of heaven as the perfect comic end to the human drama. The climax of heavenly joy will be the experience of seeing the very face of God and living joyfully in his presence forever.

Given the supreme nature of this good, any person who achieves it in the end will eventually be perfectly happy, regardless of how much he or she suffered in this life. On the other hand, any person who does not achieve it will eventually be miserable, no matter how much pleasure he or she enjoyed in this life. To be present with God in this way is the greatest possible good, and to be alienated from God is the greatest possible evil. Adams spells out the radical significance of this point for the problem of evil.

> If a face-to-face vision of God is an incommensurate good for human beings, that will surely guarantee, for any cooperative person who has it, that the balance of goods over evils will be overwhelmingly favorable. Indeed, strictly speaking, there will be no *balance* to be struck. And no one who received such benefits would have any claim against God's justice or complaint against his love. God will have bestowed on those who see him "up close" as great a good as such a finite container can take.[7]

Again, it is important to stress that the good of intimacy with God is "incommensurate" with any finite goods or evils. That means there is no way to compare or measure the joy of being in intimate relationship with infinite beauty and goodness as opposed to any finite things. The beauty and goodness of God is of such incomparable value that it will "overwhelmingly" outweigh any evils we might experience. It is like weighing the value of the world's most beautiful diamond against that of a pebble on the beach. Literally speaking, we may compare the two, but the one is so overwhelmingly more valuable than the other that, in a sense, there simply is no comparison. That is why Paul said that "the sufferings of this present time are not worth comparing with the glory about to be revealed to us."

But there is a second point that Adams develops in addition to the fact that an intimate relationship with God is an intrinsic good of immeasurable value. God also has supreme creative powers to reshape, remake, and reconfigure our lives so that they turn out to be things of extraordinary beauty, regardless of how evil has damaged us in this life. As we have already noted, evil can shatter us in a lot of ways. It can crush our spirits as well as our bodies. It can mangle our emotions and shred our psyche.

For finite beings, the damage may seem beyond repair. As Adams notes, our "meaning making capacities" are overwhelmed by horrendous evil, and we are tempted to believe that "lives marred by horrors can never again be unified and integrated into wholes with positive meaning."[8]

Think again of the little boy torn to pieces by the pack of dogs. Not only was his body torn to pieces; so also was his very *life*. It is indeed tempting to wonder how his life could ever be put back together in such a way that he would be whole again. But where human imagination and resources fail, God's infinite creative capacities do not. He can not only put his life back together; he can make of it a stunning work of art.

148

So let's return to Ivan's protest against heaven "for the love of mankind." Is it objectionable that God should put this boy's life back together since he allowed it to be shattered in the first place? Is it objectionable that God should shower upon that little five-year-old girl the sort of love she never knew existed since God allowed her parents to commit the atrocities that they did? Is it better that their lives should stand as a monument to injustice than that they should have the opportunity for God to take the broken pieces of their lives and put them back together as a thing of great beauty and positive meaning?

I do not see how anyone could maintain this protest. Indeed, I reiterate that Ivan's protest cannot claim the moral high ground it presumes to hold. Quite to the contrary, it is far better to hope that heaven is real and has the resources to overwhelm altogether whatever evils have been suffered in this life.

Okay, the Victims Are One Thing, but What about the Perpetrators?

Here it may be protested that Ivan's complaint is more about the perpetrators of treacherous evil than their victims. Even if there is some way to heal and restore the lives of those ravaged by evil, the problem remains that the perpetrators of those evils should not be forgiven. *Their* acts are so atrociously evil that it would be a moral outrage to forgive them, *ever*. And if it would be wrong for the mother whose son was torn to pieces to embrace the general, and wrong for Hugh Holliman to forgive Ricky Sanderson, then the moral objection to heaven remains.

Let's up the ante and make the objection as sharp as we can. What about Hitler, it is sometimes asked, the very godfather of unspeakable evil? Is it possible that even *he* could be saved and make it to heaven if he repented? If so, isn't the very thought of this enough to show that the Christian doctrine of heaven is a moral absurdity?

149

In a recent article, Keith Parsons appeals to the example of Hitler to show that the Christian doctrine of the afterlife is "egregiously irrational." Parsons cites his fellow atheist Eddie Tabash, who "notes that according to traditional Christian doctrine Hitler would have been forgiven had he sincerely repented and earnestly sought salvation through Christ. On the other hand, Eddie's mother, an Auschwitz survivor who died a pious Jew, has gone to hell."⁹

Now this scenario no doubt offends the moral sensibilities of many people. It does, however, point up the radical claims of the Christian gospel. Let us recall again Ivan's question: "Is there in the whole world a being who could and would have the right to forgive?" The Christian answer to this question, of course, is that there is one person, but only one, namely, Jesus Christ. He has the right to forgive first of all because he is God, against whom all sins are committed. Moreover, he is the only human being who was fully perfect, who never sinned, but who offered his life as a sacrifice so that sinners could be forgiven.

So here is the staggering good news of the gospel. Not only is it the case that *all need to be* forgiven, but *all can be* forgiven. Christ died for everyone from pious Jews to Hitler. None can be saved without him, but all can be saved by him. None can claim they do not need his grace and forgiveness, and none are so bad that they cannot be saved by his grace.

Moreover, this has a large practical implication that is most relevant to the issue at hand. Since all of us need forgiveness and Christ has extended his forgiveness to all of us, none of us are in a position to refuse to extend forgiveness to others: "Just as the Lord has forgiven you, so you also must forgive" (Col. 3:13 NRSV).

What seems objectionable about this radical teaching is that it may seem to promote "cheap grace," the notion that forgiveness comes easy and that if one is forgiven, all is automatically made right. All Hitler needs to do is accept Christ, and he is forgiven all the atrocities he committed and goes straight to heaven.

But if grace is properly understood, there is nothing cheap about it. In the first place, it was purchased at the infinite cost of the death of the Son of God and his blood, which was spilled on our behalf. We must never forget that we were redeemed not with things of finite value, like silver and gold, "but with the precious blood of Christ, like that of a lamb without defect or blemish" (1 Pet. 1:19 NRSV).

But second, it is important to understand that we are not forgiven unconditionally. To be sure, God *loves* us unconditionally, and he *unconditionally offers* us the gift of forgiveness purchased by the blood of Christ. We do not need to do anything as a condition for God to offer his forgiveness to us. However, we are not actually forgiven unless we repent and accept the offer of forgiveness.

Notice, the very act of offering forgiveness is an act of moral judgment on the person to whom it is offered. To say, "I am willing to forgive you" is to say, "You have done something wrong that needs forgiveness." To accept the offer of forgiveness is to admit the wrong. And to truly admit the wrong is to be sorry for it and to repent of it.

So a person who does not admit the need for forgiveness cannot accept it. Therefore, forgiveness is not unconditional. To actually be forgiven is conditional upon accepting the forgiveness that is offered, which requires owning the wrong that was done and turning away from it.

But a third crucial point needs to be made. Forgiveness alone is not sufficient to get to heaven. Indeed, forgiveness is only the beginning of the saving relationship with God that we need in order to live with him when heaven comes to earth. As we discussed in chapter 3, it is essential that we actually achieve "the holiness without which no one will see the Lord" (Heb. 12:14 NRSV).

If we truly understand this, we see why it is not absurd to think the mother whose son was torn to pieces could not only forgive the general but sincerely embrace him. It is not just pious imagination to say that Suzi Holliman and her father could forgive and sincerely embrace Ricky Lee Sanderson as a brother in Christ. Indeed, it is not impossible that the Jews, Poles, and Gypsies murdered by Hitler could warmly embrace him when God's kingdom has fully come.

Here is the point. Everyone in heaven will be fully transformed into the likeness of Christ. I am in no position to judge the sincerity of Ricky Lee Sanderson's conversion. But if he truly trusted in Christ and has allowed Christ to finish the work of transforming and perfecting him, there is a profoundly important sense in which he will not be the same person in heaven as the man who brutalized and murdered Suzi Holliman. Of course, he will be the same person numerically in the sense that his personal identity will be maintained, as we discussed in a previous chapter.

Like Scrooge, however, he will have come to see his entire life in the light of heaven. He will see the crimes he committed through the eyes of Christ. He will understand with full clarity the pain he caused and the wrong he did, and he will hate his sin, just as God does, and deeply regret ever committing it. To embrace this man would be like embracing Scrooge after he had become "as good a man, as good a friend" as the old city had ever seen. To embrace Sanderson in heaven would be like embracing Christ, for every redeemed person in heaven will be a "little Christ," as C. S. Lewis put it.

The same point applies to imagining Hitler in heaven. If God simply zapped him and perfected him without deep repentance on his part, it is hard to see how his moral transformation could be genuine. What is required is that Hitler come to own the truth as God discloses it to him, that he feel the pain and hurt that he caused, and that he repudiate it in the depths of his being. Such a process of thorough transformation requiring his free cooperation and willing participation would necessarily take time.

In an earlier chapter we noted that one aspect of our personal identity is the history of our choices, particularly our choices to love God and other people or not. The full story only unfolds in a temporal process. When the story is fully told, many people we could not imagine having an identity like Christ's will come to do so, perhaps even ourselves.

So again, Ivan's protest against heaven loses its moral force when we understand that final salvation requires total transformation as well as forgiveness. Heaven without purgatory is more vulnerable to Ivan's protest. But heaven with total transformation maintains the moral high ground against Ivan's protest.

But What about the Tears from Hell?

There is, however, another challenge that may be mounted against the claim that God will wipe all tears from our eyes when heaven has come to earth. Recall from chapter 2 that right in the midst of the glorious description of the new heaven and the new earth, we read about the lake of fire, which is the second death (Rev. 21:8).

Now if some persons are lost in hell and remain forever excluded from the joyful fellowship of the Holy City, would that not be the ultimate tragedy? Indeed, hell is arguably the worst part of the problem of evil. For no matter how terrible suffering may be in this life, it is finite and can be redeemed by the incomparable goodness and grace of God. But if some persons are lost forever, that represents an evil that never comes to an end and is therefore never redeemed. And if evil persists forever in this fashion, will that not produce tears that will never be wiped away?

Think about the matter in more specific, personal terms. If you are a mother, suppose your beloved child rejects God's grace decisively and remains in eternal hell. If you are a husband, suppose your beloved wife is lost, and you never see her again. Or suppose a dear friend with whom you shared many experiences and memories is lost, and you will never again see that friend or share another laugh or hug. Would that not cause sorrow and sadness? Would it not move one to weep?

Of course, every lost person is someone's child, brother, grandchild, sister, uncle, niece, or friend. But even if the persons in hell are not in any way related to you, would it still not cause you to feel pain to know they were there? Indeed, it is arguable that the more your heart is full of love, the more you would have compassion and concern for all people, regardless of whether they were personally related to you.

This argument goes back at least to the nineteenth century, when it was formulated by the German theologian Friedrich Schleiermacher. The essence of his argument as stated by contemporary philosopher Eric Reitan is that "the eternal damnation of anyone is incompatible with the salvation of any because knowledge of the sufferings of the damned would undermine the happiness of the saved."[10] In short, eternal hell is incompatible with the perfect happiness of heaven.

Now this is a difficult problem, and it is one of the more interesting arguments in favor of universal salvation. For if everyone is eventually saved, then the problem disappears. But what if we don't think universalism is a biblical option? What can we say to this challenge?

One suggestion is that those who are in heaven will no longer be aware of those who are lost. God will simply eliminate all memories of lost persons, so the suggestion goes. This however raises more problems than it solves. If memory is an important part of our personal identity, could memories of persons we have known and loved simply be erased without serious negative consequences? Consider, for instance, a close-knit family with four children. What would it be like if all memories involving the fourth child were simply erased from the memory banks of the other family members? Would not all their stories be left with inexplicable gaps? Would not their stories lose coherence? Would not part of their identity in that sense be lost?

A second suggestion is that the suffering of those in hell will not trouble us because in heaven we will have a different perspective on the damned. Randy Alcorn writes, "In Heaven, we will see with a new and far better perspective. We'll fully concur with God's judgment on the wicked."[11]

Surely Alcorn is right that we will see many things in heaven from a different perspective that will clarify things that we do not understand in this life. However, as he goes on to develop this point, he takes a direction I find more troubling. He suggests that "hell itself may provide a dark backdrop to God's shining glory and unfathomable grace." The idea here is one that a number of classical theologians have endorsed in one form or another, including Augustine and Aquinas. In their view, God's judgment on the damned will actually *enhance* the pleasures of heaven. Alcorn cites Jonathan Edwards as one who held this view.

> When the saints in glory, therefore, see the doleful state of the damned, how will this heighten their sense of the blessedness of their own state, so exceedingly different from it. They shall see the dreaded miseries of the damned, consider that they deserved the same misery, and that it was *sovereign grace*, and nothing else, which made them so much to differ from the damned.[12]

Edwards, along with Augustine and perhaps Aquinas (although this is debated by scholars), held the view most famously associated with John Calvin that God unconditionally chooses to save some persons but not others. In his "sovereign grace" he chooses to have mercy on some among the mass of fallen sinners but gives others the eternal punishment they deserve. God reveals himself even to those who are not elect, at least to some degree, but if they are not chosen for salvation by God's "sovereign grace," they will not—indeed, they *cannot*—exercise faith and be saved.

These are large and complicated issues that I have explored elsewhere, but it would take us too far afield to engage them in detail here.[13] So I will simply register my considered judgment that Alcorn's point loses its force if it is understood in Calvinistic terms. So again, consider a loved one lost in hell. God could have exercised his "sovereign grace" and saved this loved one, but he chose, for "unfathomable" reasons, to leave your loved one in sinful rebellion. He could have given this person his "irresistible grace" so that the loved one would have gladly accepted the gospel and joyfully joined the chorus of heaven in praising God. But for unfathomable reasons, God gets more glory out of his damnation than his salvation. The fundamental biblical truth that God is perfectly good and sincerely loves and wants to save all fallen sinners is completely undermined by this claim.

Rather than helping the problem, this only makes it worse—indeed, far worse. Fortunately, there is a better way to think about how the perspective of heaven will help us come to terms with hell. This was suggested by C. S. Lewis.

Sad but Not Tragic?

Let us return to the scene I discussed in chapter 3 involving Sarah Smith and her husband in Lewis's *The Great Divorce*. You will recall that she is filled with love and joy in heaven because she has allowed God's perfect love to transform her imperfect love. Her husband has taken the bus ride to heaven from hell, and she is imploring him to give up his selfish, manipulative ways so that he too can be transformed by God's love and remain in heaven. However, he remains hell-bent on using "love" to control and get his own way. He refuses to repent and chooses to return to hell under the illusion that he can hurt Sarah by doing so.

Now the narrator of the scene is distressed and expresses the opinion that Sarah Smith *should* have been more touched by the misery of her husband, even though it was self-made misery. The reply comes from George MacDonald (the nineteenth-century Scottish writer who heavily influenced Lewis), whom he meets in heaven. MacDonald acknowledges that it sounds very merciful to say that no one in heaven can be happy as long as anyone is hell.

What lurks behind that claim, however, is very troubling when we fully see it for what it is. Here it is, starkly put: "The demand of the loveless and the self-imprisoned that they should be allowed to blackmail the universe: that till they consent to be happy (on their own terms) no one else shall taste joy: that theirs shall be the final power; that Hell should be able to *veto* Heaven."[14] MacDonald goes on to point out that we cannot have it both ways. Something has to give.

> Either the day must come when joy prevails and all makers of misery are no longer able to infect it: or else for ever and ever the makers of misery can destroy in others the happiness they reject for themselves. I know it has a grand sound to say ye'll accept no salvation which leaves even one creature in the dark outside. But watch that sophistry or ye'll make a Dog in the Manger the tyrant of the universe.[15]

The image of a "Dog in the Manger" is a telling one. A manger, of course, is where the food for cattle was put. Dogs were known sometimes to get in the manger and lie down, which kept the cattle from eating. The point of the image is that the dog does not want to eat the cattle food, but by lying down in the manger and refusing to move, he keeps the cattle from eating it.

So here is the question: Should hell have the power to veto heaven? Should those who have chosen misery have the power forever to destroy or undermine the happiness they will not accept for themselves? I think it is clear that the answer is no.

Now it is important to emphasize that on Lewis's picture, the damned are given every opportunity to repent. God does everything he can to encourage them to choose heaven, short of overriding their freedom. It is not a matter of God in his "sovereign grace" passing over them in favor of others who are chosen for salvation. No, God sincerely loves everyone and truly prefers that all will be saved. The lost have elected themselves for hell; God has not done so.

So it would be wrong for good to allow evil to have veto power. Hell cannot terrorize heaven with its threats and its refusal to accept grace. This is what we will clearly understand in heaven, and that is why hell will not be able to undermine our happiness.

Here it is worth asking whether hell truly qualifies as tragic. The definition of what counts as tragic is complicated and controversial. Classically, the notion often concerned the fall of a great man who was flawed or frail in some way, and his downfall was seen as tragic because he suffered in a way that was out of proportion to his guilt. However, the tragic may also be understood more generally as anything that is very sad.[16]

Certainly the damned are not tragic heroes who suffer out of proportion to their guilt. Nor is their misery something that demands our pity, as Sarah Smith's husband would have us believe, nor is their unhappy fate due simply to frailty or weakness. To the contrary, their suffering is entirely self-chosen and only persists because of their own refusal to repent. Still, hell is very sad precisely because it involves human suffering that is in no way necessary, and in that sense it counts as tragic.

Surely, then, those in heaven will *regret* the fact that some have chosen hell and will deeply prefer that they accept grace and be saved, just as God does. This attitude of regret is a deeply moral one that springs from love and goodness. But it is precisely because it is a deeply moral attitude, one that loves goodness and righteousness, that it cannot be manipulated or terrorized by evil.

So not even the tragedy of hell can threaten the joy of heaven with tears that cannot be wiped away.

"Can It Really Be True as Religion Says . . . ?"

In conclusion, let us return to the profoundly disturbing reality that children suffer in this world, sometimes unspeakably. We have looked in some detail at Ivan Karamazov's despairing protest against heaven on behalf of suffering children. It is striking to note that the very final chapter of *The Brothers Karamazov* is also about a little boy who suffers. I wish it were the case that more people were as familiar with this chapter as they are with the far more famous chapter "Rebellion," where Ivan lodges his protest against heaven.

This final chapter is about the funeral of Ilyushechka, a frail, sickly young boy who appears fairly early in the story when Alyosha comes across a group of six schoolboys who are quarreling and throwing rocks at the little boy. Alyosha tries to intervene, but when he does so, the young boy angrily hits him with rocks and savagely bites his finger. Later we learn that Ilyushechka was so angry because the other boys had been mocking his father, who had been publicly humiliated by Alyosha's brother.

Near the end of the book, as Ilyushechka is nearing death, Alyosha patiently and lovingly reconciles the boys with him, one by one. The last boy to be reconciled is a precocious young man named Kolya, who was idolized by the other boys, particularly by Ilyushechka before the quarrel that alienated him from the others. When Kolya is finally reconciled with Ilyushechka and comes to visit him, it is especially seen as a triumph. Indeed, as they visit, it is apparent how much Kolya loves the little boy and regrets the rift that had developed in their relationship.

Kolya has never met Alyosha before this day, though he has heard much about him from the others. When he finally does, he tries to impress him with his worldly wisdom and sophistication.

He parrots the atheistic views that he has read and professes to agree with the Marxist critique of religion.

What is striking and beautiful is the contrast between Kolya as he is putting on these airs and his unpretentious and utterly heartfelt response to Ilyushechka's death. At the beginning of the chapter, we learn that Ilyushechka is especially concerned that the boys will treat his father kindly after he dies. "Papa will cry, be with papa," is Ilyushechka's dying wish.[17]

And indeed, as the funeral proceeds, Ilyushechka's parents are utterly overcome with grief and weep profusely. As Kolya witnesses their grief, his heart goes out to them, particularly the father, who had been publicly humiliated and a laughingstock the boys had mocked.

Even more significant, Kolya finds himself feeling a kind of love that dispels the pretensions he displayed when he first met Alyosha. "'You know, Karamazov,' he suddenly lowered his voice so that no one could hear, 'I feel very sad, and if only it were possible to resurrect him, I'd give anything in the world!'"[18]

Later, Alyosha addresses the boys and reiterates what a wonderful thing they had done and experienced in becoming reconciled to the little boy and in showing him their love and affection before he died. He appeals to them never to forget it and expresses the hope that what they felt that day would remain with them throughout their lives. Indeed, he assures them that if they remembered, it would give them the strength and encouragement to do the right thing on occasions when they would be tempted to do evil.

As the boys express their love for Alyosha and for each other and their resolve to remember Ilyushechka, Kolya is moved to acknowledge his hope for resurrection.

"Karamazov!" cried Kolya, "can it really be true as religion says, that we shall all rise from the dead, and come to life, and see one another again, everyone, and Ilyushechka?"

"Certainly we shall rise, certainly we shall see and gladly, joyfully tell one another all that has been," Alyosha replied, half laughing, half in ecstasy.

"Ah, how good that will be!" burst from Kolya.[19]

As I reflect on this passage, I cannot help but be reminded of Nietzsche's incredulous question we looked at in chapter 1: "Can you believe it?" He directed this question, recall, at the Christian doctrine that Christ died for us out of sheer love to pay our debt of sin. Nietzsche is not only incredulous but disdainful of the very idea that there could be a God who loves us that much. By contrast, Kolya's question is full of hope when he asks, "Can it really be true as religion says, that we shall all rise from the dead, and come to life, and see one another again?"

Despite his atheistic professions, Kolya finds himself hoping that resurrection is true. He finds himself hoping that our stories do not end at death but that "we shall see and gladly, joyfully tell one another all that has been." He finds himself hoping that our stories have a comic ending despite the fact that many episodes in this life end in tragic death.

And here we can see what may be the most profound difference of all between those who believe that ultimate reality is love and those who do not; between those who believe love is stronger than death and those who do not; between those who believe in heaven and those who do not. It is the difference between believing that even the best things of life are destined to come to a tragic end and believing that even the worst things can come to a comic end.

Heaven offers us the resources to believe that little boys torn to pieces, little girls brutalized by abusive parents, girls raped and savagely murdered, and sickly little boys who die before their life has hardly begun still have chapters of their stories yet to be written. In those chapters, they are vitally alive, they are whole, and their lives have been transformed into things of extraordinary beauty and joy. And those heartbroken parents who have wept profuse tears over the graves of their children will have those tears finally wiped away.

Even those who find this hard to believe should at least hope, "for the love of mankind," that it might "really be true."

ULTIMATE MOTIVATION

Heaven, Hell, and the Ground of Morality

The view of heaven and hell will cast a slight upon the short pleasures and pains of this present state, and will give attractions and encouragements to virtue, which reason and interest, and the care of ourselves, cannot but allow and prefer. Upon this foundation, and upon this only, morality stands firm, and may defy all competition.

—John Locke[1]

One of the most moving experiences I have ever had at the movies was several years ago when I went with my daughter to see *Les Misérables*, starring Liam Neeson. I was particularly overwhelmed by a scene in which the central character, Jean Valjean, performs a stunning act of self-sacrifice. Formerly he had been a criminal, but at the time of the scene he is the mayor of a city and a privileged man. Through the grace of others, particularly a Roman Catholic priest, along with his own efforts, he has risen above his previous life of crime to a position of distinction. He now goes by the name M. Madeleine, and his past is unsuspected by those who currently know him.

But now he must look his past squarely in the face as he observes a trial where an ignorant peasant has been mistaken for Jean Valjean and is being accused of crimes he had committed. Sitting among the other privileged spectators, he watches as witness after witness confidently identifies the peasant as the notorious criminal Valjean. Finally, when it seems evident that the man is hopelessly lost, Valjean hesitantly rises from his seat and proceeds to the center of the hall where the witnesses of the accused stood. He asks them if they recognize him, and they all shake their heads in bewildered denial. Then turning toward the jurors and the court, he speaks the riveting words, "Gentleman of the jury, release the accused. Your honor, order my arrest. He is not the man whom you seek; it is I. I am Jean Valjean."[2]

Thinking he has gone mad, the judge and the prosecuting attorney ask if there is a physician in the house. But Valjean assures them that he is fully aware of what he is doing. "I am accomplishing a duty. . . . I am the only one who sees clearly here, and I tell you the truth. What I do at this moment God beholds from on high and that is sufficient."[3] As he continues his speech, explaining his past and convincing the witnesses of his identity, clarity descends on the audience as well. What they previously viewed as a pitiful act by a deluded man they now see as a wonderful act by a man of extraordinary goodness.

In his elaboration of the scene, Hugo remarks that while nobody consciously "said to himself that he there beheld the effulgence of a great light, yet all felt dazzled at heart . . . the multitude, as by a sort of electric revelation, comprehended instantly, and at a single glance, this simple and magnificent story of a man giving himself up that another might not be condemned in his place."[4]

Hugo's description of this "simple and magnificent story" and the effect it had on those who witnessed it is a vivid picture of the power and beauty of sacrificial actions. There is a quality about them that dazzles our hearts, stretches our minds, and strengthens our resolve. We instinctively admire such actions and are often deeply moved by them. Indeed, I recall being so moved by this scene that I put my head down in my lap and wept.

Why *Should* I Be Moral? Looking to Heaven for an Answer

Most people in the greater part of human history would readily resonate with Hugo's story and immediately identify with the feelings he describes in his account. One of the most telling measures of contemporary culture, however, is that many people are dubious about such actions.

The technical name for sacrificial actions of the sort we have been thinking about is "altruism." What is remarkable about contemporary culture is the fact that the very possibility of altruistic actions is questioned by a number of noted philosophers and scientists. Altruism, it is alleged, is not what it appears. Indeed, it is quite a different thing than it is cracked up to be.

In what follows, I want to take altruism as a point of entry to discuss some dilemmas in recent moral philosophy and to suggest how heaven can help us resolve these dilemmas. Indeed, I shall argue that we need heaven to answer an even more fundamental question, namely, *Why should I be moral anyway?* Again, for most of our cultural history, it was taken for granted that we should be moral. Now, however, many people openly question what used to be taken for granted. I will argue that the same reasons we have for being moral also help us make sense of altruism and honor it, as we are naturally inclined to do.

To put the point another way, what I am seeking is a satisfactory account of deeply persuasive moral motivation.

Such moral motivation is motivation that flows out of our deepest convictions about what is ultimately true. To put it another way, deeply persuasive moral motivation is enhanced and strengthened as we reflect upon and understand what morality is and where it comes from. It will make sense of why we have moral obligations in the first place and why we should honor them. In what follows, I will argue that the doctrines of heaven and hell are vital to an account of ultimate reality that makes sense of moral obligation and why we should indeed be moral.

In saying this, I do not mean to deny that most atheists and naturalists are committed to morality and feel the force of moral demands. Indeed, atheists have offered numerous theories of moral obligation and accounts of why we should be moral that do not involve God or an afterlife.[5] Many naturalists themselves concede, however, that morality, at least as traditionally understood, is an odd thing in a naturalistic universe. Indeed, I shall argue that when we reflect on the naturalist account of ultimate reality, if we believe it is true, our moral motivation may be undermined.

So, in short, it's hard to make sense of traditional morality if naturalism is true and the human story will end tragically. But if heaven is the end of the story, morality makes a lot more sense.

The Big Dilemma of Recent Moral Philosophy

A good place to begin exploring why heaven is vital to morality is a landmark volume in moral philosophy from the nineteenth century, namely, *The Methods of Ethics* by Henry Sidgwick, a work that went through seven editions between 1874 and 1907. The author of this volume identified what he considered to be the greatest moral problem of his time, a problem he called the "Dualism of Practical Reason."[6]

Here is how the problem arises. Suppose someone is faced with a situation in which she can choose to act in a way that will promote her own personal happiness but not the happiness of the larger community. Or she can choose to act in a way that will promote the happiness of the larger community but at the cost of her own personal happiness. Which way should she choose? Is there a clear-cut answer?

Consider the concrete case of a young soldier who is called upon to put his life on the line in battle. Like other young men, he has dreams of marriage, a family, and a meaningful and successful career. But as he goes into battle, he faces the very real possibility that he might lose his life, thereby sacrificing all his dreams. Why is he willing to do so? So that other persons may be protected from aggression and have the freedom to pursue *their* dreams of happiness.

Is it rational for this young man to be willing to make this sort of sacrifice? Most of us would not only say yes, but we would consider this a deeply admirable act of great moral worth, one that deserves our deepest respect. However, would it also be reasonable if he declined to make such a sacrifice and chose instead to "look out for number one" and his own prospects for happiness?

This is the dilemma that Sidgwick identifies as the Dualism of Practical Reason. As he puts the point, it is "no less reasonable for an individual to take his own happiness as his ultimate end." The duality, then, consists in the fact that in some cases it is reasonable to pursue one's personal happiness and also reasonable to act for the happiness of others, but one cannot do both.

Sidgwick goes on to observe that in classical moral philosophy it was believed that it was good for the individual himself to act sacrificially even when the consequences as a whole are painful to him. Now this is a rather odd claim, at least on the face of it. How could it be good for *the individual himself*—however good it may be for others—to make the sort of sacrifice that brought him more pain than happiness?

In Sidgwick's view, part of the explanation is that those who believed this were simply confused. However, more significant, he also thought it was due to a "faith deeply rooted in the moral consciousness of mankind, that there cannot be really and ultimately any conflict between the two kinds of reasonableness."[7] In other words, despite what may seem to be the case, we do not have to make a choice between our own personal happiness and doing what is moral, even when that requires us to make great sacrifices for others.

But again, how could this be the case? Surely many people have been called upon to make enormous sacrifices, including the sacrifice of their dreams and even their very lives. While it is clear that *others* may benefit from their sacrifice, it is much less clear how their sacrifice advances *their* own happiness and the fulfillment of *their* dreams.

Rejecting God and Embracing Disappointment

Sidgwick returns to this unresolved difficulty in the final pages of his book. Significantly, he identifies one clear way of resolving it that he rejects, namely, by assuming the existence of God. If we assume the existence of God, he could guarantee sanctions that would be sufficient to assure it was always in our best interests to be moral. He could make certain that good was ultimately rewarded and evil punished.

He rejects this assumption, however, because he does not believe it is strictly required to ground morality. In his view, the fundamental truths of morality are as independently self-evident as the axioms of geometry and therefore need no grounding from theology or other sources. Our moral duty is intuitively obvious and clearly binding on us.

But while our moral duty is intuitively obvious, it is not equally evident that the performance of our duty will be suitably rewarded. Admittedly, we hope this will be the case not only for ourselves but for all other people as well. However, the fact that we wish this to be the case does not in any way make it probable. As Sidgwick points out, there is a "large proportion of human desires that experience shows to be doomed to disappointment."[8]

Now even if this desire is doomed to disappointment, this gives us no reason to abandon morality, according to Sidgwick. We are still obligated to do what we clearly see to be right. But it does mean we must give up the hope of making full rational sense of morality. Our moral duty is still binding on us despite the fact that it makes no rational sense how we can be obligated to do things that conflict with our overall personal self-interest and happiness.

What Sidgwick recognized as the most profound problem of moral philosophy in his day has only intensified in later generations. In much twentieth-century moral philosophy, the conflict was stated in terms of "egoism versus altruism," and morality was often defined in terms that exclude egoism or self-interest.[9] To be truly moral is not to be concerned about personal happiness and self-interest.

Moreover, this view remains widespread as moral philosophy advances into the twenty-first century. As many people see it, choosing to be moral is one thing; pursuing personal happiness is another thing altogether. It may be disappointing that we cannot do both, but that's life, and we have to suck it up and deal with it.

An Urgent Practical Question

This poses a very urgent practical question: if people are forced to choose between morality and self-interest, which are they likely to choose? If the choice is personal happiness or doing what is right, which one will win out when push comes to shove?

The issues posed by this split between morality and self-interest touch on all aspects of our common life and are consequently too pressing to be confined to the halls of academic debate. It is no surprise that these questions have worked their way into popular culture and conversation. A few decades ago, in the midst of a series of highly publicized scandals in American culture, *Time* magazine did a cover story simply entitled "What's Wrong."

These scandals epitomized the sad reality that at all levels of our society, people were ignoring moral standards in pursuit of their own advantage. This was happening in every sector of society, from business to the military to the government to the church. The same headlines, unfortunately, have been all too common in every decade of recent history.

In his analysis of what was wrong, the author of this article identified in his final paragraph a profound ambivalence in the American soul. America, he noted, was deeply double-minded, even as the nation sought to restore some sense of moral integrity: "The longing for moral regeneration must constantly vie with an equally strong aspect of America's national character, self-indulgence. It is an inner tension that may animate political life for years to come."[10]

The tension that the author notes is, of course, another variation on the same problem Sidgwick struggled with in the nineteenth century. There is, on the one hand, a longing for moral regeneration and integrity but, on the other hand, a strong tendency toward self-indulgence. Notice also that the author predicted that this tension would likely animate political life for years to come. This was written in 1987. It is safe to say that the tension is far from resolved and has likely only intensified in the years since.

In an accompanying essay, *Time* probed the roots of our moral disarray. Again, the essay ends by grappling with the relationship between morality and self-interest. The urgent practical question is whether it is possible both to be ethical and to get what we want at least most of the time.

When the question is put this way, it lays bare the heart of the problem, namely, the nature of human desires. The problem comes down to what we want and what we are willing to do to get it. With this in mind, the final sentences of the essay offer us this diagnosis of what we need for moral renewal:

> If Americans wish to strike a truer ethical balance, they may need to re-examine the values that society so seductively parades before them: a top job, political power, sexual allure, a penthouse or lakefront spread, a killing on the market. The real challenge would then become a redefinition of wants so that they serve society as well as self, defining a single ethic that guides means while it also achieves rightful ends.[11]

So what is the way out of our moral dilemma that pits morality against self-interest? Well, we simply need to redefine what we want so that we can serve society as well as self.

Now this is a remarkable prescription for curing what ails us. We just need to change what we want! Unfortunately, it begs some obvious questions. *Why* should we do so? What could possibly motivate such a redefinition of wants? Some convincing account needs to be given of goods that are clearly more desirable than money, sex, and power. The question is whether there are any goods that have this sort of value, and if so, what are they?

Moreover, are these goods the sorts of things we can choose without being forced to decide between our own ultimate self-interest and that of others? What sorts of goods might fit the bill? If there are no convincing answers to these questions, this suggestion is nothing more than an idealistic pipe dream.

When Altruism Is Severed from Self-Interest

When altruism is pried apart from self-interest and the two are seen to be at odds, it is very revealing to note that both are inevitably distorted in the process. We can see this by looking at a couple of views about the nature of self-sacrifice in contemporary thought.

One of these maintains that altruism is utterly void of any shred of self-interest whatsoever. This view is captured in the claim that the only real gift is one that expects nothing in return. A true gift is one that is given with no thought or hope of ever being reciprocated.

Continental philosophers Emmanuel Levinas and Jacques Derrida, for instance, hold the view that the highest gift one can give is a sacrifice of one's life for others—a sacrifice that is ultimate and completely uncompensated. Nothing is expected or given in return. Indeed, on this view, it is the utter finality of death that makes morality a serious matter.

So on this view, the hope of life after death is not a positive thing for morality. Quite to the contrary, the hope of heaven actually corrupts true morality. As John Milbank concisely describes this view, "Death in its unmitigated reality permits the ethical, while the notion of resurrection contaminates it with self-interest."[12] Notice, any thought of self-interest contaminates and spoils genuine morality.

On this view, altruism has been stripped of any vestige of human self-interest and raised to truly heroic proportions. This account of altruism takes moral sacrifice far beyond anything that traditional moralists imagined could be required or reasonably expected of human beings. These thinkers demand that human beings be moral superheroes prepared to make the ultimate sacrifice without any hope that there is an afterlife where goodness is rewarded and evil is punished.

Morality and Altruism as Useful Illusions

Another telling contemporary account of altruism is represented by Michael Ruse and Edward O. Wilson. They maintain that nature, particularly the evolutionary process, has made us believe in a moral code that obligates us to put self-interest aside and help others. "In short, to make us altruistic in the adaptive biological sense, our biology makes us altruistic in the more conventionally understood sense of acting on deeply held beliefs about right and wrong."[13]

In other words, we have been hardwired by evolution to believe in moral obligation, including the obligation to act self-sacrificially. Since we are hardwired in this way, we are utterly sincere when we practice altruism or admire it in other persons. It is because we consciously believe in morality in this sense that it has a positive effect on us and leads us to behave in ways that promote human survival and social flourishing.

Despite the sincerity of our deeply held moral convictions, however, the reality is that we are under the spell of a powerful illusion. We are in fact profoundly mistaken and, indeed, deceived. But this illusion serves a positive purpose according to Ruse and Wilson, as their following remarks indicate: "In an important sense, ethics as we understand it is an illusion fobbed off on us by our genes to get us to cooperate. It is without external grounding. Ethics is produced by evolution but not justified by it, because, like Macbeth's dagger, it serves a powerful purpose without existing in reality."[14]

Notice again that morality is a massive illusion since it falsely leads us to believe it is objectively true and binding upon us. But it is a beneficial illusion since the fact that we naturally believe that morality has an objective grounding is what makes us respect it and try to follow it.

This illusion also explains why ordinary people do not view morality merely as something "fobbed off on us by our genes to get us to cooperate." Nor do they view altruism as merely the product of our biology that helps the human race adapt and survive. To the contrary, they sincerely but falsely believe it is an objective reality that we are honor-bound to admire and emulate.

Which Leads Us to the Deeper Issue . . .

This brings us to another issue in contemporary moral philosophy, the big one that underlies those we have been discussing. That issue is the ultimate origin of ethics. What is the true account of the moral obligation, and where does it come from? What, if anything, gives morality its authority?

According to Wilson, centuries of debate come down to these two fundamental options: either moral principles exist outside the human mind and are independent of human experience, or they are inventions of human minds. Wilson labels those who hold the former position "transcendentalists" and those who hold the latter "empiricists."

Transcendentalists believe that morality is grounded in the eternal nature or will of God or, at the very least, in self-evident moral principles that any rational person can see as true. Empiricists, by sharp contrast, see moral principles as products of human biology and culture. Moral demands are really nothing more than the principles of the "social contract." These are agreements that human beings have made with each other in order to get along and preserve society. These principles have been transformed over time into requirements and obligations. As Wilson puts it, an "ought" statement is just shorthand for what society first chose to do and later hardened into moral codes.

The question of which one of these two fundamentally different views is true has far-reaching implications. Indeed, Wilson sees the choice between these two views as the current century's version of "the struggle for men's souls." How this issue is settled "will depend on which world view is proved correct, or at least which is more widely *perceived* to be correct."[15]

One aspect of this issue is particularly relevant to our concerns. The perception of the world in empiricist terms involves much more than how morality is construed. As Wilson notes, the empiricist view also has implications for how one understands religion and the quest for meaning. Human beings, he concedes, are incurably religious. They seek immortality and eternal significance; they hunger for communion and everlasting union with God that the doctrine of heaven promises to be true.

Without such hope, Wilson recognizes that human beings feel lost in a universe devoid of ultimate meaning. Unfortunately for us, of course, Wilson believes that religion, like morality, can be fully explained in terms of biology and evolutionary survival. Like morality, it is a product of human evolution and culture, but it is not objectively true. This claim, obviously, is sharply at odds with traditional religious truth claims, so the two views represent profoundly incompatible visions of ultimate reality.

In Wilson's view, then, those who desire both intellectual and religious truth face a deeply unsettling choice. "The essence of humanity's spiritual dilemma is that we evolved genetically to accept one truth and discovered another."[16] As he sees things, we must choose between the hope for transcendent meaning, which traditional religion offers, or the intellectual honesty of recognizing that science and biology tell us the final truth about our world.

In short, we must choose between an objective truth that disappoints our hopes or a subjective meaning that is appealing but false. That is a painful dilemma indeed.

Summarizing the Dilemmas

Now let us summarize our survey of some of the central issues in recent moral philosophy. What we have seen are a series of dilemmas, beginning with Sidgwick's "Dualism of Practical Reason." This poses the dilemma of choosing what is good for others, on the one hand, or what is good for oneself, on the other. This essential dilemma has been sharpened in the twentieth century as the conflict between egoism and altruism, and it has been taken as virtually axiomatic that the way of true morality is at odds with self-interest. And with altruism split completely apart from egoism, altruism has been twisted and recast into badly distorted forms. Underlying these issues is the more fundamental question of the ultimate origin of ethics, an issue that promises to be this century's version of the "battle for men's souls." As Wilson sees it, this battle poses a dilemma of choosing between intellectual truth and the hope for a deeper meaning of life.

Big Problems for Naturalist Accounts of Altruism and Morality

I agree with Wilson about the high stakes of this issue and all that hinges on it. Unlike him, I think there are powerful reasons to prefer a transcendental or supernatural account of the origin of morality. To be more specific, morality is best accounted for by deploying distinctively Christian resources, particularly the doctrine of heaven. I will argue my case by advancing three claims, the first two of which are especially closely related.

First, naturalistic theories such as those Wilson represents are hard pressed to account for altruism in a way that does not undermine the profound respect we naturally feel for altruistic actions, which are among the most admirable and beautiful aspects of morality. Recall what I said at the beginning of the chapter about deeply persuasive moral motivation. This is motivation that is strengthened and enhanced by reflective awareness of the ultimate origins of morality and our sense of moral obligation. I will contend that the more clearly one understands and affirms such naturalistic accounts, the less motivation one has to act altruistically.

Second, and in the same vein, naturalism is hard pressed to provide a persuasive account of genuine moral obligation. This is not to deny that it can explain why we have *feelings of*

176

obligation, but it is another matter altogether to show we *really are obligated* to behave morally.

To bring these difficulties into focus, recall the role that deception and illusion play in evolutionary and sociobiological explanations of altruism. The question this obviously raises is, what is left to motivate altruism when one finally sees through the illusion of morality? Even more to the point, what is left of altruism itself when clarity descends and one understands with reflective awareness where this tendency toward self-sacrifice comes from? If the naturalistic account of the origin of altruism is true, it can hardly be thought of in the same way it has been in traditional moral philosophy.

The same analysis applies to the naturalistic accounts of our sense of moral obligation that we have been examining. This sense of obligation depends on what many naturalists take to be a false belief, namely, that there is an objective ground of morality. Our moral convictions are thus misguided insofar as they are generated by this illusion.

Thus, we can grant that sociobiology holds promise of providing an entirely naturalistic way of explaining why we have deeply felt moral tendencies and even why we act on those tendencies. However, the question is whether it tends to unsettle, upon reflection, any natural sense of assurance that we *ought* to follow those tendencies or are under any real *obligation* to do so.

As Peter Singer has argued, the demonstration that a specific behavior is ultimately biological in origin may have the opposite effect than expected. "Far from justifying principles that are shown to be 'natural,' a biological explanation can be a way of debunking what seemed to be eternal moral axioms. When a widely accepted moral principle is given a convincing biological explanation, we need to think again about whether we should accept the principle."[17]

Notice, there is a fundamental difference between providing a biological explanation of why we are inclined to accept a given moral principle and showing that we *should* accept it. If the ultimate explanation is biological, it is far from obvious that such principles truly obligate us to follow them.

For a striking illustration of this point, consider the traditional moral conviction that infanticide is wrong because all human life is of sacred value. Well, a plausible biological explanation for this conviction is that it would be conducive to human survival to believe human life has sacred value. But on Singer's view, this biological explanation of why we feel this way does not mean we should continue to accept this moral principle as true. Indeed, Singer is notorious for his view that infanticide is acceptable for the first month or so after the birth of a baby.

In the same vein, Wilson cheerfully concedes that evolution cannot *justify* morality although it can *produce* it. That is why he says it serves a powerful purpose like Macbeth's dagger, even though it does not exist in reality. But the question I am pressing is how the "dagger" can continue to serve its purpose once we have seen through the fact that it is a shadowy illusion.

Heaven to the Rescue: Trinity, Altruism, and Moral Obligation

Let us turn now to consider the Christian account of the origin of morality, particularly altruism, and even more fundamentally, the ground of obligation. According to Christianity, as we discussed in the first chapter, ultimate reality is the Trinity, three divine persons who have eternally existed in a relationship of perfect love. Human beings owe their very existence to this three-person God who created them out of love for the purpose of knowing him and enjoying a loving relationship with him as well as their fellow creatures.

The fact that we were created for these relationships is part of what it means to say we are created in the image of God. It is this twofold claim about who God is and, secondarily, who we are that is the ultimate explanation we need to make sense of altruism.

English theologian Colin Gunton has suggested that the power of sacrifice to move us provides a telling clue about the nature of ultimate reality. He observes that the notion of sacrifice appears to be deeply rooted in human nature and the way we respond to the world. The fact that we instinctively and deeply admire Jean Valjean tells us something important. It supports Gunton's observation that we may plausibly take sacrifice as a nearly universal feature of our life in this world.[18]

Interpreting this fact theologically, he ventures the suggestion that sacrifice is the concrete "expression and outworking of the inner-trinitarian relations of giving and receiving" in the "inner being of God."[19] That is to say, sacrifice is a graphic picture of the inner nature of the Trinity: the eternal giving and receiving of love among the Father, Son, and Holy Spirit.

It is this God in whose image we were created, according to Christian theology. Moreover, our true happiness and fulfillment come from being brought into fellowship with this God. This is what explains our attraction to altruistic actions and why we naturally resonate in the depths of our being with acts of sacrificial love. *For sacrifice is the form trinitarian love takes in a fallen world*, whether shown through Christ himself or through members of his body, the church.

In God's eternal nature, the dynamic of "mutual and reciprocal gift and reception" is one of pure joy and pleasure, but in a fallen world such love sometimes requires costly and painful sacrifice. When we witness or receive a notable act of costly love, we are drawn to it because it is an earthly reflection of the eternal joy for which we were created. It is an image of the sacrificial love that God has for us, and he desires that we receive it for the sake of our deepest well-being.

In other words, it is a foretaste of heaven!

Now notice the heavenly implications for moral motivation. The more clearly we understand that sacrifice is a foretaste of heaven—the more we recognize that the eternal love of God is a matter of both gift and reception—the more motivated we are not only to respect altruism but also to act with unselfish love when there is a need for us to do so. Reflective awareness of this account of ultimate reality not only sustains but deepens our moral motivation.

To put the point another way, these beliefs provide rational reinforcement for our instinctive moral feelings. This is a significant observation for the obvious reason that we also have feelings and desires that are contrary to moral action. If rational considerations do not support morality but even undermine its rational credentials, it is likely that our moral commitments may be unsettled by thoughtful reflection and awareness.

This underscores the importance of my next point, namely, that Christian claims provide an intelligible and persuasive account of how moral obligation has an objective supernatural ground. We are obligated to be moral because morality is an expression of the will of a personal being to whom we owe our very existence. Because ultimate reality is personal and has such a will, morality is as deeply rooted as it could possibly be.

Our sense of moral obligation is consequently not illusory in any way. To the contrary, it mirrors the reality that we are essentially related by creation to a personal God and that we are forever accountable to that relationship. Moral obligation is thus far more deeply grounded in the very nature of things than it could ever be if its ultimate sources are biological, social, or cultural.

Back to Jean Valjean

To see this point, let us return for a moment to the scene from *Les Misérables* that we considered at the outset of this discussion.

Recall that the observers of the scene initially felt pity for Jean Valjean because they thought he was insane. Only after he assured them that he saw clearly what he was doing and was telling them the truth did their reaction change to profound admiration. Notice also his words, "What I do at this moment God beholds from on high and that is sufficient." Valjean's belief that he was accountable to God was at the heart of what motivated his actions. Moreover, his clarity and self-awareness about the nature of his motivation are essential to the admiration we feel for his act of self-sacrifice.

Suppose Valjean had been a naturalist who had been convinced of sociobiological explanations of morality and had offered such an account of his action. Suppose he had made this speech:

> Evolution has built into me the desire to speak the truth even when it is costly. Furthermore, it has reinforced this tendency with an illusory sense that morality has a supernatural authority behind it. This sense has been further hardened by powerful cultural and social factors over many generations. And that is sufficient.

Would we continue to admire him, or would we feel a sense of bewilderment—or even pity?

Accounting for morality in terms of heavenly truth claims not only allows us but inspires us to admire the Jean Valjeans of the world without suspecting they are mad or misguided in any way. We can do so because on this view the gift of sacrifice is given ultimately to a God of love who delights in giving us more than we can ever give in return. This trinitarian God takes pleasure in the obedient sacrifices of his children and openly promises to reward them in the life to come.[20]

In his encyclical on moral theology, Pope John Paul II notably cast the whole discussion in light of the Christian hope of heaven and eternal life. He described martyrs as those who have "obediently trusted and handed over their lives to the Father, the one who could free them from death."[21] This description highlights the fact that altruistic actions are not easy for Christians just because they believe God will reciprocate their gifts of love. Those who offer such gifts are still required to sacrifice genuine goods of this life, and it takes an act of profound trust in God on the part of those who do so to hand over their lives to God in this fashion.

Reconciling Egoism and Altruism with Heavenly Goods

This brings us to the third reason to prefer the Christian account of the origin of morality, namely, that it provides powerful resources to resolve the dilemmas that have plagued moral philosophy for the past two centuries. Notice in the first place that Sidgwick's "Dualism of Practical Reason," which fossilized in the twentieth century as the conflict between egoism and altruism, is simply dissolved by the Christian doctrine of heaven. Indeed, it is an impossible dilemma from a Christian standpoint. The fundamental reason for this is because the ultimate good for all persons is an eternal relationship with God that will climax in heaven. To enjoy this relationship, we must trust and obey God even when it is costly and difficult.

Now at the heart of what God requires of us is that we love others selflessly, but paradoxically, our own self-interest is best served when we do so. To understand this point, it is vitally important to distinguish between *self-interest* and *selfishness*.

One is acting selfishly when one promotes one's interests at the unfair expense of others. Christian morality, like most secular morality, would reject this sort of behavior as wrong. But there is nothing wrong with acting out of self-interest since all rational creatures naturally and inevitably desire their own happiness and well-being. To love another person is to promote that person's happiness and well-being. The same thing that makes it right to promote these for other persons makes it right to desire these for oneself as well. For all human beings share essentially the same nature and are equally valuable to God as creatures he loves.

Learning to love selflessly transforms us and prepares us to enter the fellowship of the Trinity in heaven. So as we love in this fashion, we are being prepared to experience our own highest joy and satisfaction. Consequently, the conflict between acting for our own ultimate good and that of others simply cannot arise.

Notice, this also provides an answer to what the author of the second *Time* magazine article I cited was looking for. Recall that that article suggested that we needed a redefinition of our wants so that they would serve society as well as self. We need something more desirable than a top job, political power, sexual allure, and a killing on the market. Well, I am arguing that the only sorts of goods that will fit the bill in a convincing fashion are heavenly ones.

If naturalism is true, the goods of this life are the only ones available, and it is a utopian fantasy to think that we can consistently act in such a way as to promote these goods both for ourselves and for others. But things are altogether different if ultimate reality is the Trinity, if giving is mutual and reciprocal in the end.

Moreover, because trinitarian love is the deepest reality, the notion of altruism as ultimate sacrifice with no expectation of compensation is at best a distortion of ultimate reality and truth. At worst, the notion that such utter disinterest represents a higher or more admirable standard is pagan hubris. As previously observed, this view is represented in current thought by such writers as Levinas and Derrida. Similar notions were expressed by the Stoics in antiquity, and in the modern period Kant is no doubt the high watermark of philosophers who worried that morality would be contaminated by any element of self-interest.

In Christian thought, resurrection and the hope of heaven
are not afterthoughts, nor are they postulates to salvage morality from irrationality. They are integral to the grand claim that
ultimate reality is reciprocal love. Christ's resurrection, no less
than his giving his life as a sacrifice for our sins, is a picture for
us of the eternal dynamic of divine love. It is life, not death—as
Levinas and Derrida contend—that gives morality substance.
As John Milbank concisely puts it, "Resurrection, not death,
is the ground of the ethical."[22]

Consider in this connection the book of Hebrews, which
presents a theologically rich account of how Christ offered his
life as a sacrifice to save us from our sins. In two passages particularly relevant to our current discussion, we are informed
not only that Christ yielded obedience to the one who could
save him from death but also that it was for the joy set before
him that he endured the cross (Heb. 5:7; 12:1–3). Thus, the
consummate sacrifice that gives meaning to all others according to the book of Hebrews gives no credence whatever to the
pagan notion that the finality of death is necessary for ultimate
sacrifice. To the contrary, the ultimate sacrifice in human history, the sacrifice that saves the world, was given in faith that
joy will triumph over death.

In commending Christ as a model in this regard, this passage is encouraging Christians who suffer for their faith to do
so with confident hope that the God whose nature is love will
reciprocate their costly obedience. Self-interest in this regard is
a straightforward component of Christian moral motivation.
Indeed, it is a rather obvious implication of the logic of trinitarian belief that we can neither harm our ultimate well-being by
obedience to God, nor can we promote it by selfishness. There
simply is no other way to be happy and to find the fulfillment
we desire than by a trusting obedience to God.

These observations further confirm the power of Christian
theology, climaxing with the doctrine of heaven, to account not

only for why morality is objectively binding upon us but also for why any reasonable person should want to obey it. It provides an account of the ground of morality and of moral motivation that is not only rationally persuasive but also beautifully winsome, one that nothing in secular morality can even begin to emulate.[23]

In short, ultimate moral motivation comes from being loved by the ultimate lover, wanting to return that love, and thereby experiencing the ultimate joy a human being can know.

The Need to Ground Morality . . . until Heaven

Before concluding, let us return for a moment to Sidgwick. Recall that he rejected the notion of theistic sanctions for morality, confident that morality could stand on its own. As Alasdair MacIntyre puts it, he held that at the "foundation of moral thinking lie beliefs in statements for the truth of which no further reason can be given."[24] MacIntyre goes on to argue that it was this sort of view that undermined any claim to objectivity and prepared the way for "emotivism." This is the view that moral judgments are essentially a matter of subjective feeling, a view that was popular for a period in twentieth-century moral philosophy.

Subsequent moral philosophy, not to mention the moral confusion of our culture, has surely shown that Sidgwick's faith was not well founded and that morality needs a better grounding than he or his heirs have provided. I have been arguing that the theism he rejected, particularly in its orthodox Christian forms, along with its account of human nature and heavenly happiness, remains the most viable resource for resolving the problems we have inherited from him.

To summarize, I have advanced three connected arguments for the claim that Christian theology, including especially the doctrine of heaven, makes better sense of morality than does naturalism. Not only can it account for altruism in a way that reinforces our instinctive admiration for it, unlike evolutionary theory, but it also has a ready explanation of why moral obligation has an objective ground. On the Christian account of things, morality is not tarnished with the sort of deception and illusion that naturalistic accounts rely upon at certain points. Moreover, the doctrine of heaven provides moral philosophy with the resources to resolve one of the most difficult problems it has been plagued with for the past several generations, namely, the conflict between egoism and altruism. Each of these arguments has force in its own right, but taken together, they provide strong reason to prefer a heavenly account of morality to earthly ones.

In short, we urgently need to recover the moral motivation that only heaven can provide, or the moral ambivalence at the heart of our culture will surely continue and even deepen.

In conclusion, I am reminded of a comment by George Mavrodes in an article in which he argues for theses similar to the ones I have just defended. Mavrodes contends that morality makes sense in a Christian world partly because of the belief that our world is fallen. When all things are made new, however, he suggests we may anticipate an economy "more akin to that of gift and sacrifice than to that of rights and duties. If something like that should be true, then perhaps morality, like the Marxist state, is destined to wither away (unless perchance it should happen to survive in hell)."[25]

If so, morality will survive only for those who never come to know the deeper reality that underlies it, the eternal relationship of mutual love, gift, and sacrifice that we call the Trinity. In the meantime, morality needs heaven, if only until the time when heaven consigns morality to hell.

HIS MERCY ENDURES FOREVER—
EVEN BEYOND THE GRAVE?

> God forbid that I should limit the time of acquiring faith
> to the present life. In the depth of the Divine mercy there
> may be opportunity to win it in the future.
>
> —Martin Luther[1]

Probably the most famous line in Dante's *Divine Comedy*—indeed, one of the most famous lines in all of literature—is also one of the most somber lines ever written. In his account of the inscription over the gate of hell, Dante wrote the following verse.

> Before me nothing but eternal things
> Were made, and I endure eternally.
> Abandon every hope, who enter here.[2]

What makes the doctrine of eternal hell so unspeakably horrible is the claim that it "endures eternally." Those who enter hell will remain there forever. To pass through its awful gate is to leave behind once and for all every hope, every prospect of either redemption or release. "Abandon every hope, who enter here."

This frightful thought of this famous line is made all the more terrifying when we add to the picture a view that is held by many orthodox Christians, namely, that our eternal destiny is sealed at the moment of death. On this view, if one dies without a saving relationship with God, one is irrevocably lost, consigned to eternal hell with no chance of ever escaping. Moreover, such a saving relationship with God requires an explicit confession of Christ as Lord.

The claim that salvation requires confession of Christ is one that some people may think makes a difficult problem even worse. How can a belief of any kind be necessary for salvation? Does entrance into heaven really hinge on accepting the truth of a proposition?

The key to answering this challenge is to recall that the essence of heaven is a perfected relationship with God in which we come to know and love him intimately. It is joining the trinitarian dance, as I put it in an earlier chapter. Now then, if God is indeed a Trinity, and Jesus is God the Son incarnate, then a perfect relationship with God entails knowing and confessing Jesus is the Son of God. Not to accept Jesus as Lord would mean one had a fundamentally mistaken view of who God is. And this would obviously be incompatible with having a perfect relationship with God.

So there is nothing arbitrary about the traditional Christian doctrine that confession of Christ is essential for salvation. Nor can this be reduced to a mere matter of affirming a proposition, though it includes that. It is more about what is involved in a personal encounter with God as he reveals himself and his love for us. Indeed, the necessity of accepting Christ is a straightforward implication of the basic Christian doctrines that God is a Trinity and Jesus is the Son of God incarnate who died for our sins and was raised from the dead. There is no other God, so if we are to have a perfected relationship with the only God that exists, we must gladly and joyfully own what God has revealed about himself.

But still, the question persists about the fate of those who have not come to see and confess these truths in this life. Is hell their inevitable destination?

Hell Is Hopeless, but Purgatory Is Hope

Let us approach this question by considering historian Jacques Le Goff's three-word summary of the essential role of purgatory in the thirteenth century, when the doctrine was systematized: "Purgatory is hope."[3] The issue I want to explore in this chapter is the sense in which purgatory can provide hope. And does it in any sense counteract the utter hopelessness represented by hell?

By way of a preliminary answer, let us consider the account of purgatory given by Dorothy Sayers in her introduction to her translation of Dante's *Purgatorio*. Sayers, an Anglican scholar and writer who was a friend of C. S. Lewis, spelled out the essence of the doctrine in six claims in order to "clear up a number of widely current perplexities and misunderstandings about Purgatory." The second and third of these are of special interest for exploring the sense in which it may be claimed that "purgatory is hope."

> (2) Purgatory is *not* a "second chance" for those who die obstinately unrepentant. The soul's own choice between God and self, made in the moment of death, is final. (This moment of final choice is known as the "Particular judgment.")

> (3) Repentance in the moment of death (*in articulo mortis*) is *always* accepted. If the movement of the soul is, however feebly, away from self and towards God, its act of confession and contrition is complete, whether or not it is accompanied by formal confession and absolution; and the soul enters Purgatory.[4]

So here we see the sense in which "purgatory is hope." One may hope that in the very moment of death, lost souls turn to God, and instead of passing through the gates of hell to hopeless eternal misery, they go instead to purgatory.

To be sure, purgatory is not a walk in the park, as Sayers sees it. But in purgatory, a person who repented at the very last possible moment can complete her repentance, pursue the holiness that she should have pursued in this life, and eventually make it to heaven. Clearly, this is infinitely preferable to the hopeless fate of eternal damnation.

Dante gives us a striking example of such a last-second convert in the case of Manfred, the son of Emperor Frederick II, a notorious sinner who only repented when he had been mortally wounded.

> When I had suffered two strokes, mortal both,
> I sighed my soul out weeping unto Him
> Whose sole delight is always to have ruth.
>
> My sins were horrible in the extreme,
> Yet such the infinite mercy's wide embrace,
> Its arms go out to all that turn to them.[5]

The amazing breadth of "mercy's wide embrace" is made even more vivid by the fact that Manfred had been excommunicated by the church. The bishop had ordered his body to be exhumed and thrown out of the kingdom as an unholy object to be disdained. Yet in Dante's account, a man who was judged to be unholy by the bishop is accepted by God and saved. Dante continues as follows.

> Their curse cannot damn a man forever
> That the eternal love may not return
> While one green hope puts forth the feeblest sliver.[6]

Notice again this extraordinary picture of the depths of God's love and mercy. All that is necessary to be embraced by his merciful arms is "one green hope" that "puts forth the feeblest sliver."

This is a God who delights to save, who rejoices when the lost sheep is found, and who welcomes with open arms the return of the prodigal (Luke 15).

But It Is *Not* a Second Chance . . .

But there is another side to Sayers's account, namely, the claim that purgatory does *not* represent a second chance to repent after death. Although it is commonly understood that way, on the traditional account of the doctrine, purgatory is only for those who die in a state of grace. Although it is possible to repent even in the last second of life, there is no possibility of conversion after death. The choice one makes in death is final and irrevocable.

But notice the qualifier in Sayers's claim. She says that those who "die obstinately unrepentant" are forever lost. But this raises an interesting question. Are all who die without repenting "obstinately unrepentant"? Are there any persons who die without repenting but who might repent later, if given the opportunity? Consider a young person who has heard the gospel but has not repented and is instantly killed, with no warning whatsoever. Or consider the countless people who have never even heard of Christ and have not even had a chance to accept him. Are all these people "obstinately unrepentant"?

Let's make the question more concrete. Consider twin boys, John and Charles, who are seniors in college. They have been raised in a Christian home and have heard lots of sermons, but they have yet to accept Christ. They are close friends as well as brothers, and their life experiences have been virtually "identical."

For their twenty-first birthday, they received a flashy black roadster with a lot of horsepower under the hood. To celebrate, they go drinking with friends and become inebriated. On the way home, driving way too fast, they lose control of the car; it flips over several times, killing Charles, while John survives with relatively minor injuries.

At this point, let us suppose John takes this experience as a "wake-up call" and gets serious about his life. He repents, becomes very active in his church, and decides to go to seminary instead of law school as previously planned. He goes on to become a great evangelist who wins many people to Christ.

Now what about Charles? On the assumption that he died without repentance, much traditional theology would consign him to the hopeless fate of eternal damnation. But consider the matter from this angle. Is it not possible and perhaps even likely that he too would have repented had he survived the car accident? Indeed, we can go further. What if God *knows* he would in fact have repented if he had lived? According to a famous theory of God's omniscience, God not only knows all the actual choices of all people who actually live, including their future choices yet to be made; he also knows what all possible people would do in all possible situations and circumstances, including those that never materialize.[7]

So let us suppose that God knows that Charles would not only have repented if he had lived but that he would have become a great Christian songwriter and musician. Had he lived, he would have joined his brother, John, and would have won many people to Christ through his music ministry.

Now then, suppose he did not repent even in the moment of death. Does it make sense to think he is hopelessly lost? If he would have repented had he lived, is it not likely that he would repent after death if given the chance? And if he would repent, would he not be gladly received into "infinite mercy's wide embrace"?

Here, many Christians balk. Along with Dorothy Sayers, they will insist that postmortem repentance is too late, that there is no "second chance" to be saved after death. The door of repentance remains open until death, but at death it is closed forever. But the question remains why this is thought to be so.

Why the End of Life Is the End of Grace: Three Proposals

In a previous chapter, I argued, following C. S. Lewis, that the doors of hell are locked on the inside. That is to say, those in hell have chosen to shut God out of their lives, and that is why the doors of hell remain locked tight.

By contrast, those who deny that there is a "second chance" to repent after death typically think that the door to repentance is closed by God at the moment of death. Even if Charles wants to repent, God will not accept his repentance. He might repent, but if so, he repents in vain. He had his chance, but that time is over. But the question persists of why this is so. What is it about death that ends any possibility of repentance? At least three answers have been suggested.

First, it might be suggested that justice requires that there can be no repentance on the other side of the grave. This life is the time for mercy and grace, but after death is the time for judgment, and if Charles dies without repenting, justice requires his damnation. In his controversial book *Love Wins*, Rob Bell pointedly challenged this position as follows.

> God would, in essence, become a fundamentally different being to them in the moment of death, a different being to them *forever*. A loving heavenly father who will go to extraordinary lengths to have a relationship with them would, in the blink of an eye, become a cruel, mean, vicious tormentor who would ensure that they had no escape from an endless future of agony.[8]

Objections may be raised to Bell's rhetorically charged language when he says a loving heavenly father would instantly "become a cruel, mean, vicious tormentor" on this scenario. However, it does seem theologically objectionable to think God's attitude toward us would change in anything like this manner merely because we had died. There is no obvious reason why justice requires God to cease having mercy at death and to punish those who have not repented by that time.

A second suggestion goes in a slightly different direction. The argument here is that if postmortem repentance is possible, that would trivialize this life or make our choices much less significant. So the point is not that God's justice requires him to make death the cutoff point for repentance but that life is a far more serious matter and has more moral significance if that is the case. So God has good reason to limit the opportunity to repent to this life in order to dramatize just how important our choices are.

What about this argument? Well, if it is a good one, it may prove too much. For if allowing postmortem repentance would trivialize this life, the same might be said for deathbed repentance. Indeed some persons have argued against deathbed repentance for just this reason.[9] Consider again the case of Manfred, the notorious sinner, who repented only when he had been mortally wounded. If he can delay his repentance until the last moment of life, does this make his previous choices less serious?

It is hard to see how repentance after death trivializes this life and our previous choices if repentance at the last moment of life does not do so. Repentance at the moment of death would not trivialize this life, so the argument goes, but repentance the moment after death would. Can a single moment of time have this much moral significance?

This notion seems even more implausible when we take into account the fact that death comes to people at very different stages of life. Some die tragically in the early stages of life, while others die in old age. Some die having had relatively few opportunities to hear and respond to the gospel, and others have many opportunities throughout their whole life.

Consider, for instance, an inner-city teenager who has only heard the gospel a few times and dies completely unexpectedly in a drive-by shooting. Now compare his case with a man who has heard thousands of sermons and only repents on his deathbed. It seems the man in the latter case has had far more opportunities to respond to the gospel than the teenager.

A third reason given why repentance is impossible after death goes back to medieval theology. Thomas Aquinas held that repentance after death is impossible because a soul cannot change its fundamental preferences without the body. So if a person dies in sin, he simply lacks the power to repent since the soul needs the body to change its fundamental orientation. His soul is stuck, as it were, in the basic moral and spiritual direction it had at the point of death.

Now this argument will carry very little weight with dualists, who believe the soul is the essential self. The soul is the thinking, feeling, willing part of the person, and it retains its basic powers even without the body. Thus, for the dualist, there is no reason in principle that the soul could not repent after death.

But let us for the moment assume that it is true that a separated soul simply cannot repent, as Aquinas thought. Does this simply rule out any possibility of repentance after death?[10]

The Emperor Trajan's Dramatic Second Chance

Here, let us consider one of the most fascinating accounts in all of Dante's *Divine Comedy*. This account describes one of the most extraordinary examples of a "second chance" one can imagine, and it involves this notion that repentance is impossible after death because the soul cannot repent without its body.

I refer to Dante's depiction of the Roman emperor Trajan, who appears in heaven in the third part of the *Comedy*. He is there among other rulers who are honored as outstanding examples of justice. The others so honored are King David,

King Hezekiah, Constantine, William of Sicily, and Rhipeus, a Trojan hero. What is particularly interesting here is the inclusion of Trajan and Rhipeus, two pagan rulers. Indeed, Dante is most surprised to see them in heaven and wonders how it is possible that they are there.

Again, let us focus on the case of Trajan. This Roman emperor actually first appears in the second part of the *Comedy*, namely, in *Purgatorio*. There he is presented as a great example of humility, whose virtuous deeds are commemorated in stone carvings that tell his story. In particular, the stone carvings tell the story of a time he was headed off to battle and was confronted by a widow who begged him for justice to be done on behalf of her son, who had been murdered. Despite his pressing business, Trajan responded to her request before going off to war.

But Dante also alludes to an even more remarkable part of Trajan's story. There was a legend that Saint Gregory prayed for Trajan, who was in limbo, the most "pleasant" part of hell, as an unbaptized pagan. Gregory was deeply disturbed by the idea that virtuous pagans who had never had a chance to hear the gospel were consigned to hell. Apparently, he was especially bothered by the case of Trajan, whose statue he regularly saw during his walks in Rome.

As legend has it, his earnest prayers for Trajan's salvation were answered in a most dramatic fashion. Trajan was briefly raised from the dead so that his body was reunited with his soul. That enabled him to repent and exercise the saving faith that allowed him to enter heaven. Dante refers to this legend in the following lines.

> And there in stone narrated was the glory
> Of the great Roman prince, whose virtues wooed
> Gregory to conquer Heaven with oratory.[11]

Notice particularly the last line, which says that Gregory's prayers conquered heaven.

We see a similar thought in the passage I mentioned earlier, where Dante expresses amazement that Trajan is in heaven along with other just rulers. When he asks for an explanation, the legend is again recounted of how Trajan's soul was reunited with his body so that he could repent and exercise saving faith.

But here is the point I really want to emphasize. The deepest explanation of this remarkable turn of events lies in the amazing love of God. Dante describes the love of God in these memorable lines.

> *Regnum coelorum* suffereth violence
> From ardent love and living hope, which still
> Conquer God's will and beat down his defence—
>
> Not as man beats down man; Himself doth will
> To suffer conquest, who by His own love
> Conquered, comes conquering and unconquerable.[12]

These paradoxical lines give us a stunning picture of the breathtaking reality of divine love.

This love is bestowed by a God who is "conquering and unconquerable." This love is given from a position of supreme strength. God is too powerful for anyone to beat him down, the way one man conquers another. No, when God is "conquered" it is because of his own will to be conquered! It is by his own love that he is conquered.

This is a stunning thought, and indeed this is one of my favorite passages in the *Comedy*. Notice, it is "ardent love and living hope" that conquer God's will. And God delights to be "conquered" by such love and hope. His very nature is love, and he loves it when we are moved by love, for when we are, it is he that is moving us. When he is "conquered" by our loving and hopeful prayer, it is he himself who comes "conquering and unconquerable."

And indeed, as the case of Trajan shows, the mere lack of a body is hardly a problem this God of conquering love cannot conquer.

The Big Underlying Issue: How Do We Conceive of God?

Here we come to one of the most fundamental issues in this whole discussion: how we conceive of God. Is Dante's striking description of the love of God more than a piece of beautiful poetry? Is it also the sober theological truth about God? And if so, what are the implications?

Consider this statement from Sayers, describing what she takes to be Dante's view of the matter: "When every allowance is made (and Dante makes generous allowance), when mercy and pity have done all they can, the consequences of sin are the sinner's—to be borne, at his own choice, in a spirit of sullen rebellion or ready acquiescence."[13]

Notice in particular her suggestion that "*every* allowance is made" and that "mercy and pity have done *all* they can." This I think represents what many Christians believe in their heart of hearts is true of the love and mercy of God. His mercy and grace are beyond measure, and we cannot even begin to fathom it.

Here is a good way to bring into focus the theological question I want to press. Is God's primary concern only to be just, so that any who are lost are rightly condemned? Or does he truly love all persons and sincerely desire to save everyone? Does he truly love us from the heart and earnestly desire a loving relationship with all persons? Is it true, as I argued above and as Sayers's quote suggests, that eternal hell is possible only because God is love and that the doors of hell are locked on the inside? Or is it the case that God locks people in hell against their will? Are some forced to stay there because they repented too late and are simply getting what they deserve?

It is important to emphasize that there are a range of positions among those who see the issue primarily in terms of justice. On one end of the spectrum are those who hold that God unconditionally saves his elect, who receive mercy, whereas the rest are simply given justice. This, of course, is the view of classic Calvinism. Some Calvinists, however, hold that God gives everyone at least some chance to be saved, so that none are lost without having some opportunity to accept Christ and be saved. Still, the primary concern is to maintain that God is justified in consigning the lost to eternal hell.

Just Enough Grace to Justify Condemnation?

A recent interesting example of this view is a position called "accessibilism" by Terrance Tiessen. According to his position, God's saving grace is universally available so that "on at least one occasion in each person's life, one is enabled to respond to God's self-revelation with a faith response that is acceptable to God as a means of justification."[14] This is true even of those who have not heard of Christ. Moreover, all people will meet Christ personally at the moment of death and will respond to him in a way that is consistent with how they have responded to God in their lifetime. If one has responded positively to God when given the chance, that person will respond positively to Christ at the moment of death.

I emphasize again that the concern here is to maintain God's justice in condemning those who are damned. The point of this theory "is to vindicate God's justice toward people who have not heard the gospel."[15] The purpose of this "sufficient" grace is clearly *not* to save as many people as possible. Indeed, on his view, this grace is not sufficient to lead anyone to salvation. Salvation requires "further" grace that causes a positive response. So in what sense is it "sufficient"? Tiessen answers as follows: "Its sufficiency lies particularly in its being enough to justify God's condemnation."[16]

Tiessen's version of "sufficient grace" is a Calvinist theory, since the only persons who are actually saved are the elect who are given the "further" grace that causes a positive response of faith. Those not committed to Calvinism will likely remain puzzled by the notion of grace that can be sufficient to condemn but not sufficient to actually lead anyone to salvation.

However, to be fair, there are also Arminian versions of the same sort of theory. Again, the claim is that God enables everyone to respond to him in faith at some point in his or her life, perhaps in the moment of death. This grace is actually sufficient in the sense that it enables a free response of faith that will lead to salvation. Those who freely respond positively are saved, and those who respond negatively are not. However, there is no opportunity to reverse this decision after death. Still, God is just in condemning those who are lost since they had at least one chance to accept his grace and refused it.

I would characterize this view, in both its Calvinist and Arminian variations, as minimal grace. The main objective, again, is not to save as many people as possible but rather to make sure that everyone has had at least some chance to be saved so that God will be justified in condemning to hell those who are not.

Optimal Grace and a Sincere Desire to Save

Now, by stark contrast, I want to consider the alternative of what I have called optimal grace.[17] The basic idea here is that God deeply and truly loves all persons and does all he can to save all persons short of overriding their freedom. Again, God does not override freedom precisely because he is love, and the essence of salvation is a freely chosen relationship with God in which we love and obey him from the heart.

Optimal grace is that measure of grace that is best suited to elicit a positive response from us and to draw us into a loving relationship with God. Optimal grace is not an abstract, impersonal concept. To the contrary, it is a deeply personal notion. It means God knows and loves each of us as individuals and understands how best to speak to us and reveal himself to us so that we will return his love. It means that God is a sensitive and discerning lover and cares about each of us as the unique persons that we are.

Now if we consider only the circumstances of this life, it seems very unlikely that everyone has optimal grace. Many people are raised in very treacherous situations and are deprived and abused in various ways, while others are loved and nurtured in positive ways that meet all their needs. Moreover, some are faithfully and lovingly taught Christian truth, while others hear only garbled versions of the gospel—if they hear it at all.

The question is whether there is any way to level the playing field so that all can have the best chance possible to respond to the gospel.[18] But let us start with the question of why God might want to do this. And a good place to begin is with the notion we have just considered, namely, that God gives everyone some chance to respond to his revelation, and everyone encounters Christ and responds to him in the moment of death.

What I want to point out here is that this specific notion is not taught in Scripture. Indeed, Tiessen freely admits that "the proposal that we all meet Christ at death moves us beyond Scripture's explicit teaching into the speculative."[19] However, he thinks it is consistent with what we know from Scripture, so he is prepared to defend the idea because it makes sense to him of how God can be just in condemning those who are lost.

But what if we think Scripture clearly teaches that God truly and deeply loves all of us and sincerely desires our salvation? What if we believe that the God revealed in Scripture is far more interested in saving the lost than merely giving them enough grace to justly condemn them to hell? Is there not room to speculate about optimal grace, just as there is for minimal grace?

Could God Give Such Grace? *Would* He?

Let's pursue these issues further by asking two questions that will help us get to the heart of the matter. These questions bring sharply into focus how we conceive of God and how we believe he has revealed himself in Scripture:

> If God can provide all persons with "sufficient grace" that enables all persons to respond in faith and be saved, could he not also provide "optimal grace" for all if he wanted to?
>
> If God could provide optimal grace for all, and if he truly loves all persons and sincerely desires their salvation, would he not do so?

So notice: there is both a "could" question and a "would" question. *Could* God provide optimal grace, and *would* he do so if he could?

The "could" question is a question about the power and creative wisdom of God. Does he have the ability to give everyone optimal grace and thereby give everyone the best chance possible to be saved? I am inclined to think the answer to this is utterly clear. Surely a God of infinite power and wisdom could do this.

Now granted, if God gives us libertarian freedom and does not determine our choices, the sort of worlds God can create is partly up to free creatures and the choices they make. So given the reality of human freedom, it is likely not possible that everyone can receive optimal grace in the space of this life. However, if the opportunities for grace are not limited to this life, surely a God who is infinitely wise and powerful could find ways to give optimal grace to all persons.

Consider again the boy raised in the inner city who has been deprived and abused and dies a tragic death as a teenager. God could surely provide grace to make up for this deprivation, to heal the abuse, and to communicate the truth of his love to this person so that he could have the best chance possible to accept the gospel and be saved.

It is not likely that such optimal grace could be presented in a moment right before death because a truly free response of faith requires true understanding of the gospel. Given the history of deprivation and abuse in this person's life, he would likely need time for various forms of emotional healing before he would be in a position to understand the good news of the gospel and accept it. Moreover, truly understanding the gospel is typically a process that requires time, since it involves truths that are presented for us to believe and internalize. Such belief comes with a conviction of sin and reflection on the love of God, who has provided a way of salvation for us.

Most people do not believe the gospel the very first time they hear it. We are convicted of the truth of the gospel as we reflect on it and the Holy Spirit witnesses to our hearts that it is true. Coming to believe the gospel is more than a matter of believing truth claims. It is more a matter of coming to know a person and to trust and believe in him. Personal knowledge is the sort of truth that takes time to absorb.

So the big point here is that surely a God of infinite power and wisdom *could* give optimal grace to all people and give them the best chance possible to accept the truth of the gospel and be saved. Death is hardly a barrier that such a God could not overcome, as the dramatic example of Trajan shows. A God of supreme power and wisdom could hardly be stymied if it were his desire to provide optimal grace for all.

The deeper question is whether he *would*. And this takes us back to the issue I highlighted earlier. How do we conceive of God? Does he truly love all persons and sincerely desire the salvation of all, or is his primary concern only to provide sufficient grace so that those who are damned are without excuse? How we answer this question will determine whether we believe God would give optimal grace if he could.

It Sounds Good, but Doesn't Scripture Rule This Out?

Here another objection must be raised. Is it not the case that Scripture clearly rules out the notion of postmortem repentance?

Even if it is an appealing idea that seems to us to make theological sense, if Scripture says otherwise, that settles the matter. Tiessen, for instance, writes that it "would be wonderful if people did, indeed, have opportunity after death to reverse decisions that they have made during their lives." However, Tiessen thinks this opportunity is precluded by Scripture. He cites two passages in particular: "Hebrews 9:27–28 distinctly teaches that judgment follows death. Jesus's parable in Luke 13:23–30 makes a similar point: the owner of the house will close the door once and for all, and there will be no chance for people to change the decision they made when the opportunity was available during their lives. Now is the critical time."[20]

Now these texts may seem, at first glance, to rule out postmortem repentance. The first of these, especially, I have frequently heard cited whenever the topic comes up. However, I do not think these texts actually do rule out postmortem repentance, and those who take them as decisive are reading far more into them than they in fact say.

The first text says only that we die once and after this is the judgment. It does not say that the judgment is immediately after death. Indeed, according to orthodox theology, the final judgment is still in the future. So even if there is a preliminary judgment immediately after death, there is no reason to think that it is the final judgment. Nor does the text claim that one's state at the time of death is decisive for one's eternal fate. This text leaves open more possibilities than are recognized by those who cite it as proof against postmortem repentance.

The same can be said for Jesus's parable in Luke. At most, the parable may rule out postmortem conversion for those who had every opportunity to truly know Christ in this life but only came to know him in a superficial sense of the word.

The text is a stern warning against evildoers who are under the delusion that they are saved merely because they "ate and drank" with Jesus or heard some of his teaching. Jesus makes clear that such superficial acquaintance is not enough for salvation.

Moreover, these evildoers are regretful, but it is far from clear that they are truly repentant. So the text does not give us any insight about how true repentance might be received. It only makes clear that presumption is foolish and that genuine salvation requires more than mere acquaintance with Christ and his teaching. That seems to be the point of the parable rather than any sort of claim about postmortem repentance.

Now then, if there are positive theological reasons in favor of postmortem repentance for those who believe that God truly loves all persons and desires their salvation, and no clear scriptural evidence that precludes it, where does that leave us? I would suggest that postmortem repentance is a theological proposal that deserves serious consideration.[21]

Indeed, I would propose that the doctrine of purgatory be amended to include this claim. This is a natural amendment that is very much in keeping with the traditional notion that "purgatory is hope." The ultimate ground of this hope, of course, is the immeasurable mercy and grace of God. An amended doctrine of purgatory allows us to give theological articulation to that hope even beyond the barrier of death. The same God whose mercy is such that he welcomes sincere repentance in the last moment of life is the God who would rejoice at the sincere repentance of a sinner after death.

Extending Purgatory Hope: Three Protestant Examples

Now some readers may find this proposal both interesting and attractive but hesitate to accept it because they consider it a theological novelty. In response to this concern, it is very much worth noting that a number of Protestant theologians have gestured in this direction as a way of thinking about purgatory that they could endorse. And as we shall see from one of these, the proposal has roots in both Scripture and patristic sources, so it is far from a mere theological novelty. Let me mention just three of these Protestant theologians.

The first example comes from nearly a hundred years ago, namely, the Scottish theologian P. T. Forsyth. He proposed a Protestant variation of purgatory in a pastoral context where he was dealing with grieving parents whose sons had been killed in World War I. Forsyth offered hope to these parents by suggesting that these heroic young men would have a chance to repent in the life to come. He wrote as follows:

> It [a heroic death] does not save. Yet it may be the moment of his conversion. It may open his moral eyes. It may begin his godly sorrow. It may be the first step in a new life, the beginning of repentance in a new life which advances faster there than here. We threw away too much when we threw purgatory clean out of doors. We threw out the baby with the dirty water of its bath. There are more conversions on the other side than on this, if the crisis of death opens the eyes as I have said.[22]

There is a certain ambiguity as to when he thinks conversion occurs. But at best, having one's moral eyes opened is only the beginning of conversion, and conversion proper can take place after death, according to this suggestion. Again, Forsyth sees the doctrine of purgatory as a good vehicle for articulating this hope.

A contemporary example is the Reformed evangelical theologian Donald Bloesch, who believes that there is an interim state (Sheol in the Old Testament and Hades in the New Testament) in which those who die outside the faith await the resurrection and coming judgment. Bloesch argues that there is support from both Scripture and patristic sources for the belief that persons in this interim state will have a chance to be converted. He cites in this connection the doctrine that Christ descended into Hades when he was killed and the view held by a number of church fathers that he preached the gospel to the dead and offered them salvation. He agrees with these patristic sources that Christ's descent into Hades opened the door of salvation to those not yet in the family of God. Bloesch states quite explicitly his belief in postmortem repentance and salvation: "It is my contention that a change of heart can still happen on the other side of death. Nothing can separate us from the love of God, not even sin and damnation (Rom. 8:38–39), and God's love goes out equally to all (Matt. 5:45; John 3:16)."[23]

And like Forsyth, moreover, Bloesch connects this suggestion with the doctrine of purgatory: "I believe that the restoration of hades as an intermediate state in which we wait and hope for Christ's salvation may speak to some of the concerns of those who embrace purgatory."[24]

It is important to emphasize that Bloesch has little sympathy for the more traditional idea of purgatory as an intermediate destination that is needed for some of the converted before they will be ready to enjoy heaven. Again, he invokes the doctrine as a way of making theological sense of postmortem conversion.

For one more example, let us turn again to C. S. Lewis. As we saw in an earlier chapter, Lewis affirms the doctrine of purgatory as a matter of completing the sanctification process in the afterlife. We have also seen that on Lewis's view, the doors of hell are locked on the inside. Now, these ideas taken together suggest that Lewis too saw some connection between the doctrine of purgatory and postmortem repentance.

Lewis dramatized his picture of the doors of hell being locked on the inside in his book *The Great Divorce*. As noted in an earlier chapter, the premise of that book is that a number of "ghosts" from "the grey town" take a bus ride to heaven and are not only invited but implored to stay. Contrary to what we would expect, most of them choose to return to hell.

At one point in the story, the narrator asks George Mac-Donald (the nineteenth-century Scottish theologian who had a big influence on Lewis), who is serving as his guide, whether the ghosts really can stay in heaven. Is there actually a way out of hell? McDonald answers as follows: "It depends on the way ye're using the words. If they leave that grey town behind it will not have been Hell. To any that leaves it, it is Purgatory."[25]

The suggestion here is that the lines between hell and purgatory are somewhat blurry if the doors to hell are locked on the inside.[26] Anyone who wants to leave the "grey town" and embrace true repentance and transformation can do so, and for them the "grey town" is purgatory. Only those who persist forever in keeping the doors locked tight remain in the "grey town," and for them it is hell.

But Wouldn't This Lead to Universalism?

Another objection we should consider before concluding this chapter is one I have often heard raised against the idea of optimal grace, which is the worry that it would lead to universalism. If there is opportunity to repent after death, everyone will repent and no one will end up in hell.

Now this is a very interesting and telling objection. Notice, it assumes that the only way anyone will remain in hell is if God is less gracious and merciful than he might be. So to make sure universalism is not true, there can be no postmortem repentance, or certainly not optimal grace that gives everyone the best opportunity possible to be saved. Indeed, I have sometimes heard this objection raised by persons who have themselves heard thousands of sermons and have benefited from every apparent advantage when it comes to Christian teaching. They object to the idea of a "second chance" for fear that if everyone had the same opportunity for salvation that they have had, no one would end up in hell.

Now here I have to ask, what would be so bad about that? Indeed, would that not be an end most to be desired? And should not those who have been given much grace and opportunity be the first to wish the same for others?

I ask these questions as one who has written not only numerous articles but also a full book defending the doctrine of eternal hell. I find myself in the somewhat odd position that I would be delighted if one of the things I have given the most energy defending in my career turned out to be false.

Let me clarify what I mean. The doctrine of eternal hell is an entirely contingent truth on my view. That is to say, I only believe it is true because I believe Scripture teaches that some persons will in fact freely and persistently resist the grace of God and be lost. If I am wrong in following this interpretation of Scripture, it is an open question whether all will be saved. Certainly *in principle all could be saved*, since Christ died for all and God sincerely desires all to be saved.

Moreover, it is emphatically not the case on my view that God *needs* some to be damned in order for him fully to be glorified, as some Calvinists apparently think.[27] God's glory is hardly threatened or diminished in any way if all are saved. Again, it is only because I believe Scripture teaches that some will decisively reject his love that I believe hell is eternal.

To put the point another way, eternal hell is not true due to the fact that some persons have little or no opportunity to be saved or far less opportunity to be saved than others. No, eternal hell is due not in any way to the *lack* of grace and opportunity but rather to the *rejection* of grace and opportunity. To insist that eternal hell must be true, even if this requires that some persons receive little or relatively little opportunity to be saved, is to place the doctrine on a very dubious foundation.

Back to the Fundamental Question

I have been arguing in this chapter for the idea of postmortem conversion as an implication of the idea of optimal grace. By contrast, the view that represents what I have called minimal grace rejects the possibility of repentance after death. Postmortem conversion allows us to make sense of how optimal grace can be given to all persons, whereas without postmortem conversion, minimal grace is perhaps the best that can be provided for many people.

I have suggested that underlying these disagreements is a deeper difference, namely, of how God is conceived. Underlying the idea of optimal grace is the conviction that God deeply and sincerely loves all persons and heartily desires the salvation of all. By striking contrast, the minimal view of grace sees God as primarily concerned with giving each person at least one chance to be saved so that he can be justified in condemning them to eternal hell.

The difference between these two views can hardly be exaggerated. But it is interesting that many Christians affirm the *rhetoric* of optimal grace but then stop short of actually affirming it in *substance*. They happily extol the boundless love of God and his amazing grace. They gladly join the psalmist in praising the mercy of God that endures forever. They heartily agree with Dorothy Sayers's statement above that God's mercy and pity do all they can, and every allowance is made to save lost sinners. They delight in Dante's description of a God who delights to have his defense beat down by love and hope, a God "who by His own love conquered, comes conquering and unconquerable."

However, when the logic of these claims leads to postmortem repentance, they draw back and affirm a position closer to minimal grace than optimal grace. Consider, by contrast, these bracing words of Donald Bloesch.

> The gates of the holy city are depicted as being open day and night (Isa. 60:11; Rev. 21:25), which means that access to the throne of grace is a continuing possibility. The gates of hell are locked only from within (C. S. Lewis). Yet even when we find

ourselves prisoners in the inner darkness that we have created, Jesus Christ has the keys to this hell and can reach out to us by his grace (Rev. 1:18). Even when one is in hell one can be forgiven.[28]

I have reiterated a number of times my agreement with C. S. Lewis that the doors of hell are locked on the inside. But Bloesch is right, I think, to frame this point with the contrasting observation that the gates of the Holy City remain open day and night. And more hopeful still is the profound truth that Jesus has the keys to hell.

The God whose mercy endures forever is a God we may hope never tires of putting his keys in the lock and bidding those within to leave it behind, naming it purgatory as they turn their faces toward the gates of heaven.

CONCLUSION

"Can You Believe It?"

Hence will arise an unmixed state of holiness and happiness
far superior to that which Adam enjoyed in paradise. . . .
And to crown all, there will be a deep, an intimate, an un-
interrupted union with God; a constant communion with
the Father and his Son Jesus Christ, through the Spirit; a
continual enjoyment of the Three-One God, and of all the
creatures in him!

—John Wesley[1]

In the final episode of the *John Adams* miniseries from HBO,
President Adams speaks of his deeply beloved wife, Abigail,
who had recently died: "I cannot conceive that God would create such a creature as her simply to live and die on the Earth."[2]
Adams lived during the period of modernity when intellectuals
were increasingly rejecting traditional Christian belief, including the doctrine of the afterlife. Adams, however, retained deep
Christian sensibilities, and these are reflected in his poignant
statement about the death of his wife. If there is a God of love,
he thought, it is inconceivable that death could be the end of
her story. Indeed, if he did not believe in an afterlife, he would
not believe in any sort of God at all.

213

Recall again the extraordinary claims Christianity makes about the love of God and the implications of that love for the life to come. Here is a passage from the great Puritan theologian Richard Baxter that vividly drives this point home.

> Is it a small thing to be beloved of God? . . . Christian, believe this and think on it. Thou shalt be eternally embraced in the arms of that love, which was from everlasting, and will extend to everlasting; of that love which brought the Son of God's love from heaven to earth, from the earth to the cross, from the cross to the grave, from the grave to glory . . . that love will eternally embrace thee. When perfect, created love and most perfect, un-created love meet together, O the blessed meeting![3]

In the first chapter, I pointed out that Friedrich Nietzsche thought the Christian doctrine of immortality absurd, a thing to be scorned. Nietzsche's attitude about life after death could hardly be more sharply at odds with that of Adams. There I suggested that the deeper issue underlying Nietzsche's sensibility was his inability to conceive of a God who loves us as deeply as the Bible assures us he does. Here again are his words: "God makes himself the ransom for what could not otherwise be ransomed; God alone has power to absolve us of a debt we can no longer discharge; the creditor offers himself as a sacrifice for his debtor out of sheer love (can you believe it?), out of love for his debtor."[4]

Although Nietzsche could not believe it, we should at least give him credit for grasping what a radical, astonishing claim Christianity makes about God and his love for us.

Postmodern Suspicion and Shriveled Hope

Indeed, I cannot help but wonder whether his incredulous question "Can you believe it?" lays bare the deepest taproot of post-modern suspicion. As much as they might want to believe it, wary postmodernists suspect that this sort of love is a massive illusion. They fear it is only a beautiful mask that will inevitably be stripped away, exposing the disappointing truth that lies behind it.

It is not hard to see why postmodernists are skeptical. Even when we have experienced real love of the human variety, it is frail, flawed, and finally fleeting. Not only does death take away the persons we dearly love, but almost everyone in contemporary Western society has been touched in one way or another by divorce and has felt the disillusionment of love that does not keep its promises. Most people enter marriage with high hopes and the best of intentions that their love will not only endure but flourish and continue to delight "until death do us part." Far too often, however, they fail to sustain the love they thought would last forever, and in the wake of their disappointment they may lose faith in love itself. It is hard to maintain trust in something that raises such soaring hopes that all too frequently come crashing down long before death intervenes.

Still, we are creatures of hope, and the fact remains that one of the most telling measures of what we dare to hope is what we find incredible. Do we find it inconceivable, as Adams did, that human beings and the relationships they cherish are made only to be broken, that they shall perish forever in the dust of death? Or are we inclined to agree with Nietzsche that it is inconceivable that the Christian account of love could be true? Is it beyond belief that there could be a God of infinite power and wisdom who loves us so much he was willing to die for us?

How we answer these questions will determine what sort of happiness we can hope to achieve. Those who find a God of love inconceivable will naturally resort to hopes that are severely diminished and shriveled compared to biblical hope.

As we have seen, Christianity is realistic about our fallen world, but at the same time it is undeniably a religion of irrepressible hope, as epitomized by its doctrine of heaven. Indeed, Christian faith audaciously bids us to intensify our hopes and enlarge our desires. It fires our imagination with visions of happiness and fulfillment beyond our wildest dreams. Reality, we are assured, outstrips our imagination—it is vastly more wonderful and beautiful than we have yet to conceive.

By glaring contrast, I was recently struck by this description of secular hope:

> The conflict between scientific naturalism and various forms of antireductionism is a staple of recent philosophy. On one side there is the hope that everything can be accounted for at the most basic level by the physical sciences, extended to include biology. On the other side are doubts about whether the reality of such features of our world as consciousness, intentionality, meaning, purpose, thought and value can be accommodated in a universe consisting at the most basic level of physical facts— facts, however sophisticated, of the kind revealed by the physical sciences.[5]

These lines come from Thomas Nagel's remarkable little book *Mind and Cosmos*, a book that challenges the reigning orthodoxy of scientific naturalism and reductionism.

Nagel himself is a committed atheist, but he is highly dubious about the dogma that all of reality can be explained in terms of the physical sciences. "The world is an astonishing place," he writes, "and the idea that we have in our possession the basic tools needed to understand it is no more credible now than it was in Aristotle's day."[6] Indeed, the aspects of reality that are the most interesting and immediately accessible to us are the very features of reality that most resist scientific explanation, things like consciousness, reason, objective moral truth, and meaning. Still, Nagel seeks an explanation of these "astonishing" features of reality in atheistic terms.[7]

But here is what strikes me about the quote above. Notice in particular this line: "There is the hope that everything can be accounted for at the most basic level by the physical sciences."

When I read this line I want to cry out, "Why would anyone *hope* this?"

Let me be clear. I can, at one level, understand regretful atheism. I can empathize with those who reluctantly come to the conclusion that God does not exist, that it's all matter and energy determined by mindless, heartless laws of nature—that the same laws of nature that somehow generated human life will eventually destroy all of us as the stars burn out and the physical remains of the universe go on expanding and disintegrating forever.

But what I cannot understand is why anyone would celebrate this vision of reality or *hope* that it is true. Why would anyone be delighted to think that when we have mastered all the laws of physics, when we have learned everything there is to know about biology, we will have gotten to the bottom of reality? Why would anyone be excited to conclude that there is nothing more to know or to give meaning to our lives? To regretfully come to this conclusion is one thing; to enthusiastically embrace it is another thing altogether. To celebrate it with a sort of triumph makes no rational, moral, or emotional sense.

It is one thing to believe your wife has a brain but not an eternal soul. It is another thing to be glad about it. It is one thing to think her most heartfelt, loving thoughts toward you are ultimately reducible to chemical events in her brain, but it is quite another thing to savor that "thought." It is one thing to believe death is stronger than love and will get the last word. It is another thing altogether to relish this prospect as a matter of hope.

Think again of President Adams when he lost his beloved Abigail. What if his faith in a loving God had wavered under attacks from modernist skeptics? What if he had said, "I hope these skeptics are right, and everything can be accounted for without God. Indeed, I hope she has met her final end, for I cannot conceive of her living beyond this life on earth"? Would you not find this a bewildering thing to *hope* for?

The Shadow of Boredom

But there is another deep root of contemporary shriveled hope that must be acknowledged, and this may explain why many people might actually wish that everything can be explained in biological and physical terms. I refer to the fear of boredom that haunts contemporary culture, a fear so prevalent that it even casts a shadow over the hope of heaven. Just as we fear that love cannot last, so we fear that neither can joy.

This is, I want to emphasize, a relatively recent phenomenon. Carol Zaleski has noted this, quipping, "Our ancestors were afraid of Hell; we are afraid of Heaven. We think it will be boring."[8] According to historian Gary Scott Smith, worries that heaven might be boring first emerged in the United States after the Civil War. "Until then, life for most people involved constant work and little entertainment, and few expressed fear that heavenly life might be monotonous, dull or routine."[9]

A culture with ample time on its hands and an obsession with entertainment is one conditioned to fear that boredom is the inevitable end of every pleasure, no matter how initially exciting it may be. Better in that case to live in a world of finite expectations where everything can be explained in terms of biology and physics, where we can get to the bottom of everything and eventually see through it as purely natural phenomena. A life that goes on forever is a terrifying thought if it cannot outrun boredom.

The boredom challenge has been answered by a number of responses, starting with the fundamental Christian conviction that God is an infinite being who has endless aspects of himself to reveal to us. Another suggestion is that God in his infinite creativity could provide never-ending patterns of enjoyable activities and pleasures that would never grow old. And there are others as well.[10]

These responses are helpful for blunting the boredom challenge, but at the end of the day I suspect the deeper issue is a variation on Nietzsche's question. Can we believe there is a God who is an eternal fountain of joy and happiness, whose very nature is to be ecstatically happy? Can we believe that the delights of love have no end? If such a God exists, eternal happiness is not only a possibility but a reality.

Perhaps our fear of boredom is a telling indicator of how far we have fallen from God and what he intends for us. If so, then heaven holds out the hope that time will not be measured by growing old and losing the vitality and zest for life. Rather, it will be measured by growing ever closer to God and sharing ever more deeply in his boundless joy and energy. To believe in God is to believe not only that love is stronger than death but also that joy is stronger than boredom.

I have been arguing in this book that the Christian doctrine of the afterlife has strong rational credentials as well as emotional appeal. The trinitarian vision of heaven is a powerful idea that can help us resolve problems ranging from the nature and ground of moral obligation to the problem of evil. It holds out the hope that even the worst of things can come to a glorious end rather than the best of things coming to a tragic end. It provides a rich account of personal identity and a deeply satisfying account of the meaning and purpose of our very lives. Even the doctrine of eternal hell makes rational and moral sense when understood in the light of this vision.

When we reflect on the existential significance of these issues, it is no exaggeration to say that to be bereft of faith in heaven is a loss of incalculable proportions for our very humanity.

All of this should be taken into account when we answer Nietzsche's incredulous question, "Can you believe it?" And if we do take it into account, I think it is clear that we ought not only hope that the Christian account of the afterlife is true but that we may heartily believe that it is. Perhaps we should even think it inconceivable that it is not.

NOTES

Introduction

1. Blaise Pascal, *Pensées*, trans. A. J. Krailsheimer (London: Penguin, 1966), 156.

2. *Harvard Theological Review* 78 (1985): 381–98.

3. Cited by Kenneth L. Woodward, "Heaven," *Newsweek*, March 27, 1989, 54.

4. Alan E. Bernstein, *The Formation of Hell: Death and Retribution in the Ancient and Early Christian Worlds* (Ithaca, NY: Cornell University Press, 1993); Jonathan L. Kvanvig, *The Problem of Hell* (New York: Oxford University Press, 1993).

5. See William Crockett, ed., *Four Views on Hell* (Grand Rapids: Zondervan, 1992); Edward William Fudge and Robert A. Peterson, *Two Views of Hell: A Biblical and Theological Dialogue* (Downers Grove, IL: InterVarsity, 2000); Robin A. Parry and Christopher H. Partridge, eds., *Universal Salvation? The Current Debate* (Grand Rapids: Eerdmans, 2003).

6. Rob Bell, *Love Wins: A Book about Heaven, Hell, and the Fate of Every Person Who Ever Lived* (New York: HarperOne, 2011).

7. April 25, 2011.

8. Lisa Miller, *Heaven: Our Enduring Fascination with the Afterlife* (New York: Harper, 2010), xix.

9. By Todd Burpo, with Lynn Vincent (Nashville: Thomas Nelson, 2010).

10. By Eben Alexander, MD (New York: Simon & Schuster, 2012).

11. See the entirety of Pascal's *pensée* number 427, from which the quote is taken.

12. *Hell: The Logic of Damnation* (Notre Dame, IN: University of Notre Dame Press, 1992); *Heaven: The Logic of Eternal Joy* (New York: Oxford University Press, 2002); *Purgatory: The Logic of Total Transformation* (New York: Oxford University Press, 2012).

Chapter 1: Heaven, Trinity, and the Meaning of Life

1. J. R. R. Tolkien, *The Lord of the Rings: The Fellowship of the Ring* (New York: Ballantine, 1954), 307.

2. Historian Gary Scott Smith suggests that contemporary concern with personal happiness has led to superficial views of heaven. See his *Heaven in the American Imagination* (New York: Oxford University Press, 2011), 214–15.

3. *Nicomachean Ethics* 1097b20.

4. Blaise Pascal, *Pensées*, trans. A. J. Krailsheimer (London: Penguin, 1966), nos. 133–34.

5. John Wesley, *The Works of John Wesley*, ed. Albert C. Outler (Nashville: Abingdon, 1986), 3:100.

6. Directed by Todd Solondz (Lionsgate, 1998). Potential viewers should be forewarned that the film contains some very disturbing material.

7. Dante Alighieri, *The Divine Comedy 3: Paradise*, trans. Dorothy L. Sayers and Barbara Reynolds (London: Penguin, 1962), 33:145 (canto 33, line 145; further quotations from Dante are cited using this format).

8. C. S. Lewis, *Mere Christianity* (San Francisco: HarperSanFrancisco, 2001), 175.

9. Wesley, *Works*, 3:101.

10. For a philosophical argument for the claim that the existence of a good God implies the existence of heaven, see Jerry L. Walls, "It Is Reasonable to Believe in Heaven and Hell," in *Debating Christian Theism*, ed. J. P. Moreland, Chad Meister, and Khaldoun A. Sweis (New York: Oxford University Press, 2013), 523–28.

11. Alvin Plantinga, *Warranted Christian Belief* (New York: Oxford University Press, 2000), 317. See also Randy Alcorn, *Heaven* (Wheaton: Tyndale, 2004), 338–40.

12. Not all agree that there will be no sex in heaven. See Colleen McDannell and Bernhard Lang, *Heaven: A History* (New York: Vintage, 1990), 261–64.

13. N. T. Wright, *Surprised by Hope: Rethinking Heaven, the Resurrection, and the Mission of the Church* (New York: HarperOne, 2008), 148.

14. Ibid., 148–52.

15. C. S. Lewis, *The Problem of Pain* (San Francisco: HarperSanFrancisco, 2001), 144. For Lewis's larger discussion of this issue, see pp. 140–47.

16. See Wesley's extraordinary sermon "The General Deliverance," in *Works*, 2:436–50.

17. See Alcorn, *Heaven*, 378–81; for his larger discussion of the issue of whether animals will be in heaven and his argument that they will be, see pp. 373–90.

18. Susan Nieman, *Evil in Modern Thought: An Alternative History of Philosophy* (Princeton: Princeton University Press, 2002), 203.

19. Thomas Aquinas, for instance, thought the resurrected body would add to the happiness of heaven, although relatively little. He wrote, "It should be said that although the body contributes nothing to the activity of the intellect by which the essence of God is seen, still it can impede it. Therefore, the perfection of the body is required in order that it not impede the lifting up of the mind." *Selected Writings*, ed. and trans. Ralph McInerny (London: Penguin, 1998), 533. He also suggests that social relations with friends will add little to heavenly happiness; see 535–36.

20. Ben Witherington III, *Revelation*, New Cambridge Bible Commentary (Cambridge: Cambridge University Press, 2003), 225.

21. *Heaven*, 170.

22. This is one of the central points of C. S. Lewis's book *The Four Loves* (New York: Harcourt Brace Jovanovich, 1960).

23. *Warranted Christian Belief*, 318.

24. The two primary images by which heaven has been imagined in literary sources are a city and a garden, both of which, of course, are inspired by the description of heaven at the end of Revelation. See Alister E. McGrath, *A Brief History of Heaven* (Oxford: Blackwell, 2003).

25. Directed by Nora Ephron (Warner Bros., 1996).

26. See C. S. Lewis, *Miracles* (San Francisco: HarperSanFrancisco, 2001), 275–81.

27. Friedrich Nietzsche, *The Antichrist*, trans. Anthony M. Ludovici (Amherst, NY: Prometheus, 2000), 59.

28. Friedrich Nietzsche, *Thus Spake Zarathustra*, trans. Walter Kaufmann (New York: Penguin, 1954), 32.

29. Ibid., 41.

30. Alcorn, *Heaven*, 405.

31. Friedrich Nietzsche, *The Birth of Tragedy* and *The Genealogy of Morals*, trans. Francis Golffing (New York: Anchor, 1956), 225.

32. Ibid., 169.

33. Ibid., 178.

34. Ibid., 179.

Chapter 2: Consolation Measures When the Dream Has Died

1. Blaise Pascal, *Pensées*, trans. A. J. Krailsheimer (London: Penguin, 1966), no. 165.

2. Bertrand Russell, *Why I Am Not a Christian*, ed. Paul Edwards (New York: Simon & Schuster, 1957), 107.

3. Bertrand Russell, *The Selected Letters of Bertrand Russell*, ed. Nicholas Griffin (London: Routledge, 2001), 2:85.

4. Russell, *Why I Am Not a Christian*, 111.

5. Ibid., 109.

6. Ibid., 62.

7. Ibid., 56.

8. Ibid., 59.

9. Richard Taylor, "The Meaning of Life," in *The Meaning of Life*, 2nd ed., ed. E. D. Klemke (Oxford: Oxford University Press, 2000), 175.

10. Thomas Nagel, "The Absurd," in Klemke, *Meaning of Life*, 183.

11. Ibid., 185.

12. Keith Parsons, "Seven Common Misconceptions about Atheism," 1998, http://www.infidels. org/library/keith_parsons/misconceptions.html#motive.

13. Ibid.

14. Pascal, *Pensées*, no. 200.

15. Cited in Carl Sagan, *Billions and Billions: Thoughts on Life and Death at the Brink of the Millennium* (New York: Random House, 1997), 221.

16. Ibid., 215.

17. Cited in John Polkinghorne, "Eschatology: Some Questions and Some Insights from Science," in *The End of the World and the Ends of God*, ed. John Polkinghorne and Michael Welker (Harrisburg, PA: Trinity Press International, 2000), 32.

Chapter 3: If God Is Love, Why Is There a Hell?

1. C. S. Lewis, *The Great Divorce* (San Francisco: HarperSanFrancisco, 2001), 75.

2. C. S. Lewis, *The Problem of Pain* (San Francisco: HarperSanFrancisco, 2001), 130.

3. John Wesley, *The Works of John Wesley*, ed. Albert C. Outler (Nashville: Abingdon, 1984), 1:554; 2:76–77, 80.

4. Here I slide over a complex issue, namely, why finite creatures require moral freedom to be good, whereas God does not. For insightful discussion of this issue, see Joshua Rasmussen, "On the Value of Freedom to Do Evil," *Faith and Philosophy* 30 (2013): 418–28; and Kevin Timpe, *Free Will in Philosophical Theology* (New York: Bloomsbury, 2014), 103–18.

5. Rob Bell, *Love Wins: A Book about Heaven, Hell, and the Fate of Every Person Who Ever Lived* (New York: HarperOne, 2011), 113.

6. Marilyn McCord Adams, *Horrendous Evil and the Goodness of God* (Ithaca, NY: Cornell University Press, 1999), 157.

7. Thomas Talbott, "Freedom, Damnation and the Power to Sin with Impunity," *Religious Studies* 37 (2001): 417.

8. Ibid., 427.

9. Thomas Talbott, "Misery and Freedom: Reply to Walls," *Religious Studies* 40 (2004): 218.

10. Ibid., 221–22.

11. Talbott, "Freedom, Damnation," 417.

12. This question was posed by Matt O'Reilly on Rachel Held Evans's blog.

13. David Bentley Hart, *The Beauty of the Infinite: The Aesthetics of Christian Truth* (Grand Rapids: Eerdmans, 2003), 399.

14. Personal correspondence with the author in an email, January 18, 2014. Mulholland made this observation in response to my asking whether the spring of life and the fire of hell might be contrasted as I have suggested. See also Mulholland's discussion of Revelation 14 in his commentary on Revelation in the Cornerstone Biblical Commentary: *James, 1–2 Peter, Jude, Revelation*, ed. Philip W. Comfort (Wheaton: Tyndale, 2011).

15. Lewis, *Great Divorce*, 122–24.

16. Ibid., 129.

17. Ibid., 130.

Chapter 4: If We Are Saved by Grace, Why Do We Need Purgatory?

1. Dorothy L. Sayers, introduction to *The Divine Comedy 2: Purgatory*, by Dante Alighieri (London: Penguin, 1955), 16.

2. John Calvin, *Institutes of the Christian Religion*, ed. John T. McNeill, trans. Ford Lewis Battles (Philadelphia: Westminster, 1960), 3.5.6.

3. Cited by Roland H. Bainton, *Here I Stand: A Life of Martin Luther* (New York: Abingdon-Cokesbury, 1950), 78.

4. See *Credo* 3, no. 1 (January 2013).

5. John Fletcher, *Checks to Antinomianism* (New York: Hunt & Eaton, 1889), 2:488.

6. For a recent defense of the Roman Catholic view of purgatory that attempts to show biblical support for the doctrine, see Gary A. Anderson, "Is Purgatory Biblical?," *First Things* (November 2011): 39–44.

7. Martin Jugie, *Purgatory and the Means to Avoid It*, translated from the 7th French edition by Malachy Gerard Carroll (Cork: Mercier, 1949), 9.

8. For a detailed discussion of these different models of purgatory, see chap. 3 of my *Purgatory: The Logic of Total Transformation* (New York: Oxford University Press, 2012).

9. Dorothy L. Sayers, introduction to *The Divine Comedy 2: Purgatory*, 58.

10. C. S. Lewis, *Letters to Malcolm: Chiefly on Prayer* (London: Geoffrey Bles, 1963), 139.

11. For a more detailed discussion of Lewis's account of purgatory than I have space to provide here, see chap. 6 of my book *Purgatory: The Logic of Total Transformation*.

12. C. S. Lewis, *Mere Christianity* (San Francisco: HarperSanFrancisco, 2001), 52.

13. Ibid., 56.

14. Ibid., 58.

15. Ibid.

16. A likely historical influence for Lewis's view of the atonement is the nineteenth-century Scottish theologian McLeod Campbell. For an exposition and critical analysis of this view, see Oliver Crisp, "Non-Penal Substitution," *International Journal of Systematic Theology* 9 (2007): 415–33. Crisp points out that a passage from Jonathan Edwards was the original inspiration for Campbell's work. It is also worth remarking that, while Lewis's view of the atonement lends itself readily to his transformational soteriology, his soteriology does not require his theory of atonement. I have argued elsewhere that there are several theories of atonement in contemporary philosophical theology that are amenable to a transformational view of salvation. See Jerry L. Walls, *Heaven: The Logic of Eternal Joy* (New York: Oxford University Press, 2002), 41–48.

17. Lewis, *Mere Christianity*, 57.

18. The doctrine of "imputed righteousness" is very much a matter of controversy among Protestants, particularly evangelical theologians and biblical scholars. For an important critique, see N. T. Wright, *Justification: God's Plan and Paul's Vision* (Downers Grove, IL: IVP Academic, 2009).

19. For more on these points, see Scott R. Burson and Jerry L. Walls, *C. S. Lewis and Francis Schaeffer: Lessons for a New Century from the Most Influential Apologists of Our Time* (Downers Grove, IL: InterVarsity, 1998), 51–63.

20. Lewis, *Mere Christianity*, 92; cf. 81, 118–20, 147–48, 176, 192.

21. See chapters 11 and 12 of book 3.

22. Lewis, *Mere Christianity*, 192.

23. Ibid., 192–93.

24. Ibid., 175.

25. Ibid., 177; cf. 147, 195, 199.

26. Ibid., 191–92.

27. Ibid., 198.

28. Ibid., 202.

29. Ibid., 203, 205, 212, 221.

30. Ibid., 204.

31. Lewis, *Letters to Malcolm*, 139–40.

32. Ibid., 140.

33. John Wesley, *The Works of John Wesley*, ed. Albert C. Outler (Nashville: Abingdon, 1985), 2:431.

34. Brett Salkeld, *Can Catholics and Evangelicals Agree about Purgatory and the Last Judgment?* (New York: Paulist Press, 2011), 22.

35. Chris Castaldo, "Purgatory's Logic, History and Meaning," *Credo* 3 (January 2013): 41; cf. 49.

36. John Polkinghorne, *The God of Hope and the End of the World* (New Haven: Yale University Press, 2002), 131.

37. Thanks to Joe Dongell for discussion of this text and these observations.

Chapter 5: Saving Souls and/or Bodies

1. Charles Taylor, *Sources of the Self: The Making of the Modern Identity* (Cambridge, MA: Harvard University Press, 1989), 47.

2. Dante Alighieri, *The Divine Comedy: Purgatorio*, trans. Allen Mandelbaum (New York: Everyman's Library, 1995), 2:76–87.

3. Randy Alcorn, *Heaven* (Wheaton: Tyndale, 2004), 57–59.

4. John Polkinghorne, *The God of Hope and the End of the World* (New Haven: Yale University Press, 2002), 103–7.

5. See John Cooper, *Body, Soul and Life Everlasting: Biblical Anthropology and the Monism-Dualism Debate* (Grand Rapids: Eerdmans, 1989).

6. Nicholas Wolterstorff, *Lament for a Son* (Grand Rapids: Eerdmans, 1987), 33.

7. Taylor, *Sources of the Self*, 50.

8. Joseph Ratzinger, *Eschatology: Death and Eternal Life*, 2nd ed., trans. Michael Waldstein (Washington, DC: Catholic University of America Press, 1988), 183–84.

9. Colin Gunton, *The One, the Three and the Many: God, Creation and the Culture of Modernity* (Cambridge: Cambridge University Press, 1993), 207.

10. Alasdair MacIntyre, *Three Rival Versions of Moral Enquiry: Encyclopaedia, Genealogy, and Tradition* (Notre Dame, IN: University of Notre Dame Press, 1990), 199.

11. Friedrich Nietzsche, *Twilight of the Idols and The Anti-Christ*, trans. R. J. Hollingdale (London: Penguin, 1990), 65.

12. David Brown, "No Heaven without Purgatory," *Religious Studies* 21 (1985): 451.

13. Charles Dickens, *A Christmas Carol and Other Christmas Books* (Oxford: Oxford University Press, 2006), 14.

14. Ibid., 83.

15. Ibid., 52.

16. Ibid., 24.

17. Ratzinger, *Eschatology*, 259.

Chapter 6: Wiping Away Every Tear?

1. Marilyn McCord Adams, *Horrendous Evils and the Goodness of God* (Ithaca, NY: Cornell University Press, 1999), 204–5.

2. Fyodor Dostoevsky, *The Brothers Karamazov*, trans. Richard Pevear and Larissa Volokhonsky (New York: Everyman's Library, 1992), 245.

3. Cited in Martin Tady and John Railey, "A Test of Faith," *Winston-Salem Journal*, January 18, 1998, A10.

4. Ibid.

5. Peter van Inwagen, "Quam Dilecta," in *God and the Philosophers*, ed. Thomas V. Morris (New York: Oxford University Press, 1994), 47.

6. Richard E. Creel, *Divine Impassibility: An Essay in Philosophical Theology* (Cambridge: Cambridge University Press, 1986), 149.

7. Marilyn McCord Adams, "Redemptive Suffering: A Christian Solution to the Problem of Evil," in *The Problem of Evil: Selected Readings*, ed. Michael L. Peterson (Notre Dame, IN: University of Notre Dame Press, 1992), 183.

8. Adams, *Horrendous Evils*, 148. For insightful discussion of Adams and the resources of theodicy for defeating horrors, see Philip Tallon, *The Poetics of Evil: Toward an Aesthetic Theodicy* (New York: Oxford University Press, 2012), 169–98.

9. Keith Parsons, "Heaven and Hell," in *Debating Christian Theism*, ed. J. P. Moreland, Chad Meister, and Khaldoun A. Sweis (New York: Oxford University Press, 2013), 534.

10. Eric Reitan, "Eternal Damnation and Blessed Ignorance: Is the Damnation of Some Incompatible with the Salvation of Any?," *Religious Studies* 38 (2002): 429.

11. Randy Alcorn, *Heaven* (Wheaton: Tyndale, 2004), 347.

12. Ibid.

13. See Jerry L. Walls and Joseph R. Dongell, *Why I Am Not a Calvinist* (Downers Grove, IL: InterVarsity, 2004); and Jerry L. Walls, "Why No Classical Theist, Let Alone Orthodox Christian, Should *Ever* Be a Compatibilist," *Philosophia Christi* 13 (2011): 75–104. See also my YouTube videos "What's Wrong with Calvinism": https://www.youtube.com/watch?v=Daomzm3nyIg; and https://www.youtube.com/watch?v=Wt9ENcBoMRE.

14. C. S. Lewis, *The Great Divorce* (San Francisco: HarperSanFrancisco, 2001), 135.

15. Ibid., 136.

16. For an excellent discussion of the tragic as a challenge to theodicy, see Tallon, *Poetics of Evil*, 133–67. For issues surrounding the definition of the tragic, see especially 137–42.

17. Dostoevsky, *Brothers Karamazov*, 768.

18. Ibid., 773.

19. Ibid., 776.

Chapter 7: Ultimate Motivation

1. John Locke, *The Reasonableness of Christianity*, ed. I. T. Ramsey (Stanford, CA: Stanford University Press, 1958), 70.

2. Victor Hugo, *Les Misérables* (London: Standard Book Company, 1931), 1:263.

3. Ibid.

4. Ibid., 265.

5. As I write, David Baggett and I are working on a book that critiques various naturalistic theories of morality. This volume is a follow-up to our coauthored volume *Good God: The Theistic Foundations of Morality* (New York: Oxford University Press, 2011).

6. Henry Sidgwick, *The Methods of Ethics* (Chicago: University of Chicago Press, 1962), 404n1.

7. Ibid., 405.

8. Ibid., 507–8.

9. Cf. John Rawls: "Although egoism is logically consistent and in this sense not irrational, it is incompatible with what we intuitively regard as the moral point of view. The significance of egoism philosophically is not as an alternative conception of right but as a challenge to any such conception." *A Theory of Justice* (Cambridge, MA: Harvard University Press, 1971), 136.

10. Walter Shapiro, "What's Wrong," *Time*, May 25, 1987, 17.

11. Ezra Bowen, "Looking to Its Roots," *Time*, May 25, 1987, 29.

12. John Milbank, "The Ethics of Self-Sacrifice," *First Things* 91 (March 1999): 34.

13. Michael Ruse and Edward O. Wilson, "The Evolution of Ethics," in *Religion and the Natural Sciences: The Range of Engagement*, ed. James E. Huchingson (Fort Worth: Harcourt Brace Jovanovich, 1993), 310.

14. Ibid.

15. Edward O. Wilson, "The Biological Basis of Morality," *Atlantic Monthly*, April 1998, 54.

16. Ibid., 70.

17. Peter Singer, "Ethics and Sociobiology," in Huchingson, *Religion and the Natural Sciences*, 321.

18. Colin Gunton, "The Sacrifice and the Sacrifices," in *Trinity, Incarnation and Atonement: Philosophical and Theological Essays*, ed. Ronald J. Feenstra and Cornelius Plantinga Jr. (Notre Dame, IN: University of Notre Dame Press, 1989), 215.

19. Ibid., 221.

20. The New Testament is unabashed in teaching that obedience and sacrifice will not go unrewarded. For just one example, see Matt. 19:27–30.

21. Pope John Paul II, *The Splendor of Truth* (Boston: St. Paul Books and Media, 1993), 114.

22. "Ethics of Self-Sacrifice," 38.

23. For a more detailed discussion of these issues, see chap. 7 of my *Heaven: The Logic of Eternal Joy* (New York: Oxford University Press, 2002); and chap. 10 of *Good God: The Theistic Foundations of Morality*.

24. Alasdair MacIntyre, *After Virtue*, 2nd ed. (Notre Dame, IN: University of Notre Dame Press, 1984), 65.

25. George I. Mavrodes, "Religion and the Queerness of Morality," in *Rationality, Religious Belief, and Moral Commitment: New Essays in the Philosophy of Religion*, ed. Robert Audi and William J. Wainwright (Ithaca, NY: Cornell University Press, 1986), 226.

Chapter 8: His Mercy Endures Forever—Even beyond the Grave?

1. Cited by Donald Bloesch, *The Last Things: Resurrection, Judgment, Glory* (Downers Grove, IL: InterVarsity, 2004), 146. Bloesch notes that this was more of a passing hope than an integral part of his creed.

2. Dante Alighieri, *The Divine Comedy: Inferno*, trans. Allen Mandelbaum (New York: Everyman's Library, 1995), 3:7–9.

3. Jacques Le Goff, *The Birth of Purgatory*, trans. Arthur Goldhammer (Chicago: University of Chicago Press, 1984), 306.

4. Dorothy L. Sayers, introduction to Dante, *The Divine Comedy 2: Purgatory*, trans. Dorothy L. Sayers (London: Penguin, 1955), 59.

5. Dante, *Purgatory*, 3:118–23 (trans. Sayers).

6. Ibid., 3:133–35.

7. I refer, of course, to Molina's theory of middle knowledge. William Lane Craig has appealed to this idea to solve the difficulty of those who have never heard the gospel. Craig suggests that God has arranged things so that those who never hear the gospel are all persons he knows would not have accepted it if they had heard it. For a discussion and critique of this view, see Jerry L. Walls, *Hell: The Logic of Damnation* (Notre Dame, IN: University of Notre Dame Press, 1992), 96–97.

8. Rob Bell, *Love Wins: A Book about Heaven, Hell, and the Fate of Every Person Who Ever Lived* (New York: HarperOne, 2001), 173–74.

9. For instance, see Jeremy Taylor, *The Rules and Exercises of Holy Dying* (1710; repr., Whitefish, MT: Kessinger, 2007), 145, 152, 277. Taylor insists that true repentance requires time and can only be completed at death, not begun.

10. Kevin Timpe argues that repentance after death is psychologically impossible, but he rejects Aquinas's account of why this is so. See Kevin Timpe, *Free Will in Philosophical Theology* (New York: Bloomsbury, 2014), 76–78. He admits he does not have a good philosophical reason for this but affirms it on the basis of Christian tradition.

11. Dante, *Purgatory*, 10:73–75 (trans. Sayers).

12. Dante Alighieri, *The Divine Comedy 3: Paradise*, trans. Dorothy L. Sayers and Barbara Reynolds (London: Penguin, 1962), 20:94–99. The Latin phrase in line 94 means "suffereth violence."

13. Sayers, introduction to *Purgatory*, 17. I have argued that, unfortunately, Dante does not consistently affirm the view of God's grace and mercy that Sayers depicts in this quote. See Jerry L. Walls, *Purgatory: The Logic of Total Transformation* (New York: Oxford University Press, 2012), 129–37.

14. Terrance L. Tiessen, *Who Can Be Saved? Reassessing Salvation in Christ and World Religions* (Downers Grove, IL: InterVarsity, 2004), 25.

15. Ibid., 26.

16. Ibid., 242.

17. For more on optimal grace, see Walls, *Hell*, 85–94.

18. C. S. Lewis seems to have had a similar idea in mind in his chapter "Morality and Psychoanalysis." See *Mere Christianity* (San Francisco: HarperSanFrancisco, 2001), 88–93.

19. Tiessen, *Who Can Be Saved?*, 218.

20. Ibid., 221.

21. For further discussion of these issues, see chap. 3 of my *Heaven: The Logic of Eternal Joy* (New York: Oxford University Press, 2002); Kyle Blanchette and Jerry L. Walls, "God and Hell Reconciled," in *God and Evil: The Case for God in a World Filled with Pain*, ed. Chad Meister and James K. Dew Jr. (Downers Grove, IL: InterVarsity, 2013), 243–58.

22. P. T. Forsyth, *This Life and the Next* (Boston: Pilgrim, 1948), 36–37.

23. Bloesch, *Last Things*, 146–47.

24. Ibid., 152.

25. C. S. Lewis, *The Great Divorce* (San Francisco: HarperSanFrancisco, 2001), 68.

26. For more on this, see C. P. Ragland, "Love and Damnation," in *Metaphysics and God*, ed. Kevin Timpe (New York: Routledge, 2009), 206–24.

27. See John Piper, *Does God Desire All to Be Saved?* (Wheaton: Crossway, 2013).

28. Bloesch, *Last Things*, 227.

Conclusion

1. John Wesley, *The Works of John Wesley*, ed. Albert C. Outler (Nashville: Abingdon, 1985), 2:510.

2. This quote is a paraphrase of a passage from a letter Adams wrote to Thomas Jefferson in response to a letter of condolence that Jefferson had written him. The larger passage reads as follows: "I believe in God and in his wisdom and benevolence, and I cannot conceive that such a Being could make such a species as the human merely to live and die on this earth. If I did not believe in a future state, I should believe in no God. This universe, this all, this *to pan* ["totality"] would appear with all its swelling pomp, a boyish firework." The passage is in *The Adams-Jefferson Letters*, ed. Lester J. Cappon (Chapel Hill: University of North Carolina Press, 1959), 530. Thanks to Luke Van Horn for calling my attention to the quote from the HBO series and to Chris Hammons for the original quote.

3. Richard Baxter, *The Saints' Everlasting Rest*, ed. John T. Wilkinson (Vancouver: Regent College Publishing, 2004), 45.

4. Friedrich Nietzsche, *The Birth of Tragedy* and *The Genealogy of Morals*, trans. Francis Golffing (New York: Anchor, 1956), 225.

5. Thomas Nagel, *Mind and Cosmos: Why the Materialist Neo-Darwinian Conception of Nature Is Almost Certainly False* (New York: Oxford University Press, 2012), 13.

6. Ibid., 7.

7. For an incisive critique of Nagel on this score, see David Baggett's review essay "On Thomas Nagel's Rejection of Atheism," *Harvard Theological Review* 106, no. 2 (2013): 227–38.

8. Carol Zaleski, "In Defense of Immortality," *First Things* 105 (September 2000): 42.

9. Gary Scott Smith, *Heaven in the American Imagination* (New York: Oxford University Press, 2011), 228.

10. Garth Hallett surveys six proposed solutions to this difficulty in "The Tedium of Immortality," *Faith and Philosophy* 18 (2001): 279–91.

INDEX

accessibilism, 199–200
accountability, 131–32
Acts, book of, 85
Adams, John, 213, 217, 230n2
Adams, Marilyn McCord, 74–76, 147
Alcorn, Randy, 38, 43, 124–25, 155–56
Alpha and Omega, 24–25, 27, 48–49
altruism, 169–73, 175–77, 179, 182–85,
    228n9
Antichrist, The (Nietzsche), 42
Apostles' Creed, 29–30
Aquinas, Thomas. *See* Thomas Aquinas
Aristotle, 20–22
atheism, 48–53, 144–45
atonement, 101–3
Augustine, 155

Baxter, Richard, 214
beatific vision, 37–39
Bell, Rob, 13, 73, 193
Benedict XVI (pope), 130, 138
Bloesch, Donald, 206–7, 210–11
body, the, 43–44
    and dualism vs. physicalism, 120–27
    and "intermediate heaven," 124–27
    and purgatory, 126–27
    resurrection of, 29–30, 32, 119,
        222n19
    See also identity

Brothers Karamazov, The (Dostoevsky),
    140–42, 145, 148–49, 153, 159–61
Brown, David, 133–34

Calvin, John, 155–56
    on purgatory, 91–92, 99
Calvinism, 113, 198–99
*Can Catholics and Evangelicals Agree
    about Purgatory and the Last
    Judgment?* (Salkeld), 93
Castaldo, Chris, 113–14
Christmas Carol, A (Dickens), 134–38
Colossians, book of, 150
compulsion, and repentance, 78–82
Corinthians, First, book of, 41, 125
Corinthians, Second, book of, 114,
    124–25, 146
Craig, William Lane, 229n7
creation, theology of, 29–32, 42–43
Credo, 93
Creel, Richard, 145

dancing, 43–44
Dante Alighieri, 24, 47, 122
death
    and the afterlife, 29–32, 124–25
    death of, 32–33
    identity after, 117
    repentance after, 198–208

Derrida, Jacques, 172, 183–84
Dickens, Charles, 134–38
Divine Comedy (Dante), 24, 122–24, 187–91, 195–98, 210
Dostoevsky, Fyodor, 140–42
dualism, and the body, 120–27
"Dualism of Practical Reason" (Sidgwick), 166–69, 175, 182

Edwards, Jonathan, 155
Einstein, Albert, 63
eros, sexual, 28–29
evil, problem of, 139
  and atheism, 144–45
  Christian response to, 146–49
  and heaven, 140–53, 159–62
  and perpetrators, 148–53
evolution, 172–73, 175, 177, 181
Exodus, book of, 37, 41

Fletcher, John, 95
forgiveness, God's
  and evil, 149–52
Forsythe, P. T., 206
Four Loves, The (Lewis), 87–88
fragmentation, and modernity, 33–34
freedom, 51, 73, 79–80, 108, 113
  and divine and human will, 74–76
  and hell, 69–90, 200, 202
  and repentance, 78
"Free Man's Worship, A" (Russell), 50–53

Genesis, book of, 35
grace, 115, 150–51, 158, 193, 199
  sovereign, 94, 155–56, 158
  sufficient vs. optimal, 94, 199–203, 208–11
Great Divorce, The (Lewis), 87–90, 156–57, 207–8
Gregory, Saint, 196
Gunton, Colin, 130–31, 179

happiness, 19–23
  and Alpha and Omega, 24–27
  great thinkers on, 20–23, 26–27, 110
  and heaven, 24–27, 218–19
  and love, 23–24

Happiness (movie), 22
Hart, David Bentley, 85–86
heaven, 27–28, 31, 223n24
  and being with God, 35–39
  and boredom, 218
  and culture, 34–35
  and death, 32–33
  doctrine of
    critique of, 42–44
    and problem of evil, 140–51, 159–62
    and suffering in hell, 153–58
  and Eden, 39
  and happiness, 24–27
  identity in, 117–20
  and longing, 27–29
  loss of the dream of, 47–50, 64–65
    and fleetingness of life, 58–64
    and irony, 57–58
    and meaning of life, 54–62
    Russell on, 50–53
    and Sisyphus, 53–55
  and materiality, 29–32, 38–42
  and morality, 165–66, 179–86
  and new earth, 29–32
  and sex, 28–29
  and truth, beauty, and goodness, 33–34, 47
Hebrews, book of, 93–94, 151, 184, 204
hell
  doctrine of, 208–9
  as eternal, 187–89
  as forcibly imposed punishment, 78–80, 82
    and the rich man and Lazarus, 82–84, 89–90
  as freely chosen, 86–89
  and a loving God, 67–68, 70–73, 85
    and freedom, 69–90
    logic of, 68–70
  and purgatory, 189–209
  suffering in, 79–84
    and image of fire, 85–86
    and joy in heaven, 153–58
    and the presence of God, 84–86
Hitler, Adolf, 149–53
Holliman, Hugh, 143–44, 152
Holliman, Suzi, 143, 152

Hugo, Victor, 163–65
Hume, David, 131

identity
  and character change, 133–38
  and the life story, 127–30, 133–38
  and modern thought, 131–32
  theories of, 127–30
  through death and resurrection, 117
    and dualism vs. physicalism, 120–27
    and "intermediate heaven," 124–27
    and Jesus, 117–19
    and purgatory, 126–27, 133–38
intimacy, with God, 37
  as incommensurate good, 147–48
Isaiah, book of, 31, 36

James, book of, 73
Jesus Christ, 26, 28, 32, 115–16
  and the incarnation, 36–37, 102–3
  as Lamb of God, 44–46
  postresurrection appearances of,
    117–19
  and sanctification, 106–9
  and trinitarian love, 70–72
John, book of, 26, 28, 37, 44–45, 46, 207
  and love, 70–72
John, First, book of, 26, 114
John Paul II, Pope, 181–82
Jugie, Martin, 97–98
justice, God's, 198–99
justification, by faith, 103

Le Goff, Jacques, 189
Letters to Malcolm (Lewis), 99, 109–10
Levinas, Emmanuel, 172, 183–84
Lewis, C. S., 31, 87–90
  on atonement, 101–6, 225n16
  on hell, 70, 87, 156–57, 210–11
  on purgatory, 99–103, 109–10
  on sanctification and faith, 104–9
love
  and freedom and hell, 70–73
  of God, 213–14
    and postmodern suspicion, 214–16
    and postmortem repentance, 197–
      203, 209–11

trinitarian, 70–72, 179, 183
  as ultimate reality, 44–46, 67
  See also hell: and a loving God
Love Wins (Bell), 193
Luke, book of, 84, 114, 115–16, 117–18,
  204–5

MacDonald, George, 157, 207–8
MacIntyre, Alasdair, 131–32, 185
Mark, book of, 137–38
Matthew, book of, 28, 31, 36, 207
Mavrodes, George, 186
meaning of life, without heaven, 53–57,
  64–65
  and fleetingness, 58–64
  and human intellect, 57–58
Mere Christianity (Lewis), 100–107
Methods of Ethics, The (Sidgwick),
  166–69
Michael (movie), 39–40
Milbank, John, 172, 184
Mind and Cosmos (Nagel), 216
Misérables, Les (Hugo), 163–65, 180–82
morality, 163–65
  and altruism and egoism, 165, 169–77,
    179, 182–85, 228n9
  Christian account of, 178–86
  and emotivism, 185
  and "empiricists" vs. "transcendental-
    ists," 174–76
  and evolution, 172–73, 175, 177, 181
  ground of, 168–69, 174–76
  and heaven and hell, 165–66, 179–86
  motivation for, 165–68, 171, 176–77
  and naturalism, 166, 176–77, 183
  objective vs. subjective, 52
  and selfishness vs. self-interest, 182–84
Moses, 37, 41, 84

Nagel, Thomas, 60, 216
  on irony of life, 57–58
naturalism, 216–17
  and morality, 166, 176–77, 183
Nicomachean Ethics (Aristotle), 20
Nieman, Susan, 33
Nietzsche, Friedrich, 132, 214, 218–19
  on heaven, 42–44, 161
  and "will to power," 45–46

Parsons, Keith, 59–62, 150
Pascal, Blaise, 21, 23, 61
Paul (apostle), 30, 31, 41, 79, 85, 114
  on life after death, 124–25
  on suffering, 146–47
Peter, First, book of, 45, 151
Philemon, book of, 114
Philippians, book of, 114
physicalism, 121, 124
Plantinga, Alvin, 29, 39
Polkinghorne, John, 115, 126
postmodernism, 214–16
prodigal son, the, 76–78
Protestant Reformation, 92, 96, 98
Psalms, book of, 85
purgatory
  argument for, 93–95
  as grace, 115–16
  and hell, 189–91
    and the love of God, 197–99
    not second chance, 189, 191
    and obstinate unrepentance, 191–92
    and repentance after death, 192–208
    and universalism, 208–9
  and identity, 126–27, 133–38
  Lewis on, 99–102, 109–10
  Protestant and Catholic views on, 91–99, 113
  and sanctification vs. satisfaction, 94–100, 109–15

Ratzinger, Joseph, 130, 138
Rawls, John, 228n9
reductionism, 216–17
Reitan, Eric, 154
repentance
  and compulsion, 78–82
  and forcibly imposed punishment, 78–80, 82
  as inevitable, 80–81
repentance, postmortem, 189, 191–93, 229n10
  and God becoming unforgiving, 193–94
  and the love of God, 197–205
  and purgatory, 205–8
  and Scripture, 203–5, 206–7

and soul without body, 195–97
and this life's decisions, 194–95
Revelation, book of, 45–46, 125
  on heaven, 24–27, 29–39, 49–50, 86, 93, 139, 210–11
  on hell, 68–70, 84–86, 153, 210–11
Romans, book of, 30–31, 146, 207
Ruse, Michael, 172–73
Russell, Bertrand
  and heaven, 48–53, 56
  on worship, 51

Sagan, Carl, 63–64
Salkeld, Brett, 93, 112
salvation, 188–89
  theology of, 32
  universal, 68–69, 74, 154, 208–9
sanctification, 104–6
  and Christ, 106–9
  and purgatory, 94–100, 110–15
  speed of, 94, 112–15
  and the Trinity, 106–7
Sanderson, Ricky Lee, 143–44, 152
Sayers, Dorothy, 98
  on purgatory, 189–90, 192, 198, 210
Schleiermacher, Friedrich, 154
science, physical, 216–17
Sidgwick, Henry, 166–69, 175, 182, 185
Singer, Peter, 177
Sisyphus, 54–56
Smith, Gary Scott, 218, 222n2
Socrates, 55
soul, the, 138, 195–97
Sources of the Self (Taylor), 128–29
spiritual, as nonmaterial, 40–42
suffering, and the afterlife, 79–84, 139–40, 146–47, 153–58

Tabash, Eddie, 150
Talbott, Thomas, 76–84, 86
Taylor, Charles, 127–29
Taylor, Richard, 54–57
teleology, 25–26, 131–32
Tetzel (monk), 92, 99
Thomas Aquinas, 121, 155, 195, 222n19
Thus Spake Zarathustra (Nietzsche), 43
Tiessen, Terrance, 199–201

Time magazine, 13, 170, 183
tragedy, 158
Trajan, second chance of, 195–98
Trinity, the, 70–72, 106–7, 130, 179,
    183–84, 188

Weinberg, Steven, 64–65
Wesley, John, 26–27, 31, 72, 110

Wilson, Edward O., 172–78
Witherington, Ben, 38
Wolterstorff, Nicholas, 128
"worship" for atheists, 51
Wright, N. T., 30

Zaleski, Carol, 218